QUIVERTREE
PUBLICATIONS

"Thank you for believing in yourself enough to have the guts to go out to the wider medical community, refute some of your previous work and believe so much in your new research that you are prepared to take the criticism that is bound to be thrown at you. I have struggled with weight issues since I was a 10-year-old. I have literally tried every diet known to man. The problem with all these diets was I was always constantly hungry despite eating huge platefuls of food, a problem I have not encountered with this way of eating. To say it has been a success is an understatement. I have managed to get to my slimmest ever in my entire adult life and have been able to maintain it so far." HEATHER LOCK

"Life-changing event! On the high carb diet I upped the running and nothing happened. So I dropped my calorie intake down to 1 500 calories per day and ran more but after two months I'd put on a kilogram and felt permanently tired. That is about when I saw your article and everything changed." JOHN MARTIN

"I have never had as much energy as I have now and can easily see any length of a gym session through without the need to supplement with food before I go. I feel I am finally in control of my body. I am no longer nearly as hungry as I was – so much so that I actually have to remind myself to eat. My life and conscious thought of food are forever changed. Not only mine, but also a few others who managed to see my changes and have made even more impact in their own and their families' lives. Truly a gift that keeps giving. Again, I am indebted to your work." PIETER LE ROUX

"I am 56 years old and lost 11kg in a little over two months switching to low carb high fat. Now I'm thin, muscular, and full of energy without effort. I am actually in the best shape I have been since high school and I don't even exercise significantly." DR MICHAEL MYERS

"Thank you very much for your low carb crusade. I am healthier and feel better than I have for 20 years, and it may even have saved my life." DR ANTHONY MOSHAL

"It has become very clear to me what was making me tired these last many years: the carbohydrates I've been eating all this time! My energy level is UP!" STEPHEN MOGAMI MPHOMANE

"In the past I tried a low fat diet, which proved impossible to maintain. I lasted a year on this diet and as I was perpetually hungry, so I gave it up. Eating fat has made me thin. Certainly what I have been eating for the past year is really making me healthy in that it has reversed several chronic ailments and I currently need no medication. There is no incentive for me to leave this agreeable diet. The population is becoming steadily more obese, diabetic and hypertensive despite the popularisation of the low fat diet and incentives to eat certain (low fat) foods." PROFESSOR JONNY MYERS

"Thank you for saving my life… If a scientist can't change his opinion when confronted with new evidence, then he can't call himself a scientist." NEIL ALAN EBERHARD

"I have just completed the London Marathon in 03:28:08 without carbohydrate loading, gels and a diet of less than 50gms per day. At 67 years of age it is my overall best for age marathon, and my best time for over 10 years. I believe that under three hours is more than possible for a man of my age and I have Ed Whitlock's over-70 marathon record in my sights." TIMOTHY KIRK

"Started my day with double cream Greek yoghurt, coconut oil and berries for breakfast. Water and two sachets of UCAN and a Kiri cream cheese at half way was all I had for the entire run. Finished feeling strong and took 1hr30min off last year's Comrades finishing time (9hr56min). LCHF all the way! No dips, no surges, no gastrointestinal issues, no drips, no trip in the ambulance. I am so chuffed! Thank you TIM NOAKES for educating me!" SHELLEY LIEBENBERG

"I noticed increasing muscular discomfort in early 2012, which got so severe it threatened my physical independence. I then developed frozen shoulders and multiple site tendonitis. When even steroid injections weren't effective, I tried LCHF eating. Four months later I achieved a handicap win at a 10km run, and three months after that, I completed a marathon in 4hr12min. I wonder how many patients I've treated with pills and platitudes when I should have been enquiring about their diet?" DR KERRY ALLERTON

THE REAL MEAL
REVOLUTION

CHANGING THE WORLD, ONE MEAL AT A TIME

PROF TIM NOAKES

SALLY-ANN CREED

JONNO PROUDFOOT

DAVID GRIER

CONTENTS

FOREWORD

Throughout my playing career I was always looking at ways to improve my competitive edge.

I began by emphasising my physical fitness and was one of the first to incorporate weight training into my workout routine at a time when most golfers thought I was crazy to do so. I made sure I was as fit and strong as I could be, so that when it came to the back nine of a Major on the Sunday, I knew I could remain alert.

In addition to focusing on my fitness, I also began to concentrate on the mental side of golf. I believe the mind is a critical factor in competition and can be an extremely strong differentiator.

But one of the most significant changes I made was to my nutrition.

I began to pay attention to my diet as a strong indicator of my athletic success. I saw the benefits of correct nutrition, not only in my physical being, but also in my mental state and how it allowed me to concentrate for longer and be sharper on the golf course.

Early in my career I was chided for being a "fitness fanatic". I was told there was no place or need in golf for the kind of athleticism I brought to the game. Yet, today you cannot go to a single tournament on the PGA Tour without finding a mobile gym, and the leading players work out religiously and are very cognisant of their diets.

Since I have stopped playing, I have made it my mission to educate as many people as possible about correct diet and the dangers of obesity. I have travelled the world and I have seen the debilitating effects of obesity. People are dying because they are eating incorrectly, and like it is a last supper. Children are becoming obese and sick because they are not focusing on the proper foods and are consuming processed junk that has become the norm in today's society.

So when Tim Noakes said he was busy with a "food revolution", I knew exactly what he meant.

Tim is a man I greatly admire. I have always followed his work, and I believe his effort to educate people about correct nutrition is critically important in this age. Tim is a pioneer and a man who is not afraid to challenge convention. And now he has started the food revolution, armed with the rigorous testing, analysis and research that Tim usually employs in all of his work.

The world of food and nutrition is changing. People have access to more information. They are more empowered than any generation before us to make informed choices about what they eat. And they no longer accept blindly what they're told or what's on the label.

If the biggest change you can make in your life is what you put into your body, then start today.

Make no mistake, this is a food revolution, and you have no better guide on this journey than Tim Noakes.

GARY PLAYER

We dedicate this book to each of you who – dissatisfied with average health. surplus weight and dipping energy levels – decided to take charge of your bodies and make a change. Understanding that conventional wisdom on nutrition fell flat. you opened your minds. cast aside your preconceptions and began testing the facts for yourselves. By sharing your stories and the lessons in this book you are setting in motion a groundswell movement towards a true revolution in the way we eat.

http://realmealrevolution.com

You may not feel particularly unhealthy, but we'd wager that you've become accustomed to having average health, telling yourself that weight gain and worsening athletic ability is an inevitable part of age and life. Like a car with a characteristic rattle that eventually causes the engine to fall apart, you see feeling sluggish, bloated, constipated or ravenously hungry (despite eating "well") as just part of who and how you are.

What if you could turn it all around? Lose weight, regain the ridiculous energy levels of your youth and prevent against serious killers like obesity and diabetes? How about if you could do that while still eating really well? You know… all the good stuff packed with flavour – juicy steak, eggs pretty much any way you like them, roast chicken, heavenly bacon and more?

What if you could not only eat tasty, filling food (thereby not feeling starved or restricted), but get an end result where you feel stronger, fitter and more energised than ever before, even bettering the sporting ability of what you thought was your youthful prime?

Yes? Then welcome to *The Real Meal Revolution*, a lifestyle designed to change your weight, your health and your life. This is not a newfangled diet involving bizarre strategies and supplements that you'll never be able to stick to. Rather, it's a return to your dietary roots, bringing you back to the way humans are meant to eat and returning your body and mind back to the trim, happy, energised state our ancestors experienced thousands of years ago. They didn't get fat or suffer from obesity, diabetes or other lifestyle illnesses.

Neither should you.

Vive la Revolution!

"THERE ARE NO MEAL TIMES.
NO PORTION SIZES.
NO KILOJOULE RESTRICTION.
LET YOUR BODY TELL YOU
HOW MUCH TO EAT.
THE ONLY THING YOU COUNT
IS THE GRAMS OF SUGAR OR
CARBOHYDRATES. I LOOK IN
THE FRIDGE AND
I CHOOSE THE FOOD."

Prof Tim Noakes

WHAT IT'S ALL ABOUT

Part myth-busting scientific thriller, part mouth-watering cookbook, the goal of *The Real Meal Revolution* is to change your life by teaching you how to take charge of your weight and your health through the way you eat. Like our eating patterns, when it comes to reading, some people like a tasting menu, others prefer to get to the meat of the matter and still others like to digest the full smorgasbord of information, which is why we have divided this book into three sections for you to dip into and out of at will.

It's important to note that this is not a crash diet, not a get-thin-quickly programme – but a sustainable, long-term lifestyle which will lead to steady weight loss and increasing health benefits.

For STARTERS you will get an overview to:
• Understand what it is humans are actually designed to eat and learn that far from being a new low-carb, high-fat (LCHF) diet, this was the original human eating plan long before anyone ever got fat.
• Discover how our original, ancestral eating plan got hijacked.
• Digest what the consequences of that hijacking were to our health as a species.
• Get to grips with how good fat got a bad rap.

For MAINS we get practical and:
• Learn – from Sally-Ann Creed's nutritional tips and the basics of stocking a fridge to shopping for Banting – how to set yourself up to transition from the high-carb, low-fat (HCLF) way you probably eat now, to Banting, which will help you lose weight and feel great.
• Discover how easy it is to cook the Banting way from loads of mouth-watering recipes designed by chef-athletes David Grier and Jonno Proudfoot.

For DESSERT:
• Settle in for the fascinating story behind the Banting movement as South Africa's foremost sports and exercise scientist Tim Noakes delves into the history and science behind human nutritional evolution and the three major historical catastrophes that conspired to lead us to the overweight, sickly state many of us find ourselves in today.
• Realise through South African case studies and the authors' success stories how the tide is changing as we get smart about what's really good for us.

Dig in.

MEET THE TEAM

A scientist, a nutritionist, and two chef-athletes – the crack squad behind *The Real Meal Revolution* have walked or in some cases run the hard yards through the gauntlets of nutritional science and self-experimentation. The revelatory stance and the mouth-watering recipes in this book are the result of their experience combined with overwhelming scientific evidence.

THE SCIENTIST – PROFESSOR TIM NOAKES

Tim is a highly respected South African Professor of Exercise and Sports Science at the University of Cape Town. He has run more than 70 marathons and ultra-marathons and is the author of the books *The Lore of Running, Challenging Beliefs* and *Waterlogged*. After publishing his latest book, Tim entered the dietary sphere challenging the science behind obesity, coronary heart disease and heart attacks. Tim has dedicated his later life to opening people's eyes to the myth of low-fat eating and the nutritional and environmental crisis it has now left us in.

"Working on this book, the goal is to remove the blinkers of accepted nutritional wisdom by unleashing the scientific evidence showing that the introduction of low-fat eating after 1977 is the direct cause of the twin epidemics of obesity and diabetes that began in 1980. We present the scientific evidence showing why low-fat eating is unhealthy for those suffering from insulin/carbohydrate resistance and how high-fat diets have the unique capacity to reverse all known coronary risk factors, especially in those with the most marked insulin/carbohydrate resistance. But it's not all science. Working with Sally's nutritionist knowledge and the foodie skills of Jonno and David we will show you how to apply eating the LCHF/Banting way practically in your own life through your fridge, your shopping trolley and your stove. All the ingredients are here for you to make major improvements in your weight, your health and your life."

THE NUTRITIONIST – SALLY-ANN CREED

Sally-Ann spent most of her life sick with chronic asthma, sinusitis and panic disorder, undergoing many operations on her sinuses, and spending 13 long years as a "victim" of panic disorder and agoraphobia. Through an adjustment in her diet, she regained her health and qualified as a Nutritional Therapist (Post Graduate Diploma in Clinical Nutrition, Australia). Her goal is to help others experience the same results. Having found that food and supplements could dramatically change her life, giving her the quality of life she'd always dreamed about, she decided to study so that she could help others. Her story is relayed in her best-selling book *Let Food Be Your Medicine* – an easy to understand guide to healthy living.

"*The Real Meal Revolution's* timing couldn't be more perfect. The entire world is looking at the Paleo/ Banting movement now with dozens of Hollywood celebrities adopting this way of eating with massive success. The low-carb, high-fat lifestyle is arguably the most contemporary dietary lifestyle since Atkins. Although technically not "new" Banting has been updated by current scientific knowledge giving us the best possible opportunity to revolutionise our own health. I personally changed from a low-fat, high-carb diet 16 years ago to a high-fat low-carb diet – it completely changed my life and I've never looked back: I have perfect blood levels of all the important readings, and am enjoying the best health of my life. I encourage anyone stuck in a health or obesity rut to give this a try – it may change your life too!"

THE ADVENTURER - DAVID GRIER

Over the past 30 years David has been involved in the restaurant and hospitality industry in South Africa, owning a string of successful fine dining restaurants. After all those years in the kitchen, one day someone left the kitchen door open and he bolted to follow his dream of becoming an extreme adventurer. Since this journey began he has run The Great Wall Of China (4 200km in 93 days), run the entire coastline of South Africa (3 300 km in 80 days), paddled from Africa to Madagascar (500km in 12 days), run the Island of Madagascar south to north (2 700km in 67 days) and run the entire length of India (4 008 km in 93 days). Each of these missions was embarked on in aid of David's charity, the Miles for Smiles Foundation. Funds are raised to provide corrective surgery for children born with cleft lips and palates. To date, funds raised through David's missions have given over 1 000 children the God-given right to a smile. Throughout all of David's athletic escapades, he has followed a strict, low-carb, high-fat eating plan.

"As a chef one learns the basics, but then it is up to you to take what you've learned to the next level. You need to be passionate, innovative and creative about what you are working with, but the downside for me was that the hours and the strain on the body began to add up. I managed to achieve many goals in cooking and reached the top, but in the process I ended up becoming unhealthy and overweight (110kg). I began to really look at my life and tried to change my lifestyle, but no matter how hard I tried with exercise and conventional nutrition, the results were not great. Slowly, I began experimenting with LCHF/Banting eating. Being in the kitchen, with all the temptation bubbling around me it was really hard initially to stay focused on the correct path, but then it all clicked. The results speak for themselves. To make LCHF/Banting eating work for you, you just need to be passionate, creative and most importantly, you need to want to change!"

THE CHEF - JONNO PROUDFOOT

After training and working in a five-times rated Top 10 restaurant in his early career, Jonno moved through a variety of food and wine establishments before finding his passion in Paleo and LCHF cookery. Since the birth of his interest in performance food and nutrition he has co-hosted 52 episodes of award-winning children's cooking show, *What's Your Flava*. He has also appeared as a guest chef to *cook without carbs* on the *Expresso Show* on numerous occasions.

"The low-carb lifestyle first got my attention when my girlfriend lost 19kg in less than six months after battling with her weight for many years. The term 'happy wife, happy life' became instantly significant as she looked and felt better all the time. Having had an interest in diet and nutrition, specifically sports nutrition for many years, this grabbed my attention. Seeing real results in someone after watching people struggle with weight issues my whole life immediately swayed my ways and I began Banting. The impact on my life has been significant. My physical performance has exploded. I can swim harder and longer than ever before and I no longer feel bloated and uncomfortable, before, during or after training. Eliminating my carb intake and increasing my fat has substantially reduced my appetite. Even with constant lapses in willpower, I managed to drop three notches in my belt over my first month of Banting. My concentration and focus have sharpened significantly especially after lunch when, in the past, I used to feel groggy and exhausted from a carb-rich lunch."

GLOSSARY
MEET THE TERMS:

LCHF = Low-carb, High-fat [preferred term: BANTING]
The nutritional lifestyle we advocate for *The Real Meal Revolution*. To be known henceforth as "friend".

BANTING = THE DIET NAMED AFTER WILLIAM BANTING.
The morbidly obese undertaker who was the first guinea pig of the LCHF diet, reducing his weight so drastically that his approach became known as the Banting diet. Both a verb and a noun, e.g. "Why aren't you eating any potato bake?" "I'm done with carbs, I'm Banting. I've dropped 20kg in a month and added 40kg to my benchpress."

HCLF = High-carb, Low-fat
The diet you have probably been following due to tragically unchallenged misinformation out of the USA in the 1970s. To be known henceforth as "foe".

IR = INSULIN RESISTANT
The state the majority of humans find themselves in, caused by a reduced capacity to metabolise ingested carbohydrates, safely and efficiently.

T1DM = TYPE-1 DIABETES MELLITUS
An auto-immune disease and the less common form of diabetes, occurring mainly in younger people, usually children. The immune system attacks pancreatic cells, either destroying them completely or damaging them badly enough that they're prevented from producing enough insulin. Can be genetic.

T2DM = TYPE-2 DIABETES MELLITUS
A nutritional and lifestyle disease associated with insulin resistance.

KETOGENIC DIET = A diet consisting of 25 to 50g of carbohydrates per day.

APPESTAT= An area of the brain that controls appetite.

KETOSIS = When the body switches to a very high fat-burning state, using ketone bodies (energy molecules in the blood, converted from fat by the liver) as "fuel" for the brain. Achieved by depriving the body of carbohydrates to reduce insulin in the body. Also seen as the euphoric state you reach when you rid your body of carbohydrates and your body begins using fat as fuel, reducing your appetite considerably.

CARB-FREE= Ridiculously low in carbs.

BON APPETIT = BANTING FOR "ENJOY YOUR FOOD".

SMARTER, FITTER, FATTER

What do TV science and weather guru Simon Gear and a primitive human who lived 195 000 years ago have in common? Other than basic physiological structure, they could sit down to dinner together.

Gear has always been active, yet despite regular activity, by age 25 his weight had increased to 80kg. Because of skin chafing and sore knees due to his weight, he was unable to run more than 70km/week in training. In October 2011 he decided to "reinvigorate" his flagging running career by completing nine marathons in nine South African provinces in nine consecutive weeks. The intervention failed. Instead, his weight increased by three kilos and he ran poorly. In April 2012 he completed the Two Oceans ultra-marathon in his slowest-ever time (6:57:57).

At a loss to explain his weight, Gear read Professor Tim Noakes' book *Challenging Beliefs*. Inspired, he prescribed to the "Noakes diet" and in no time, Gear's body started to transform. Within the first week he lost 2.4kg without running. Within six months he had lost 15kg. Over the next four months his training load reached 120km/week. During this training, his weight dropped by only two kilos, showing a disconnect between weight loss and calories expended.

On March 16th 2013, he completed the Two Oceans ultra-marathon in 3:59:42, an improvement of nearly three hours on his performance a year earlier. For Gear, now 37, the effect on his life, weight and running had been huge. He said, "The important point with all this was that the weight loss enabled my training, not the other way around. I feel like I have won my life back."

When Billy Tosh, 44, discovered he could no longer fit into an economy class aeroplane seat, he drove directly from the airport to his GP, who found his blood pressure (160/100mmHg) and blood glucose concentration to be raised. She advised that he begin immediate treatment for both conditions and consult a dietician. He spent the night searching the Internet, where he discovered the "Noakes diet". He adopted the diet immediately.

His weight loss began straight away and continued unchecked for seven months, during which time he lost 84.6kg. After six months he returned to his GP, who didn't recognise him. His blood pressure and fasting blood glucose and cholesterol concentrations had reverted to the normal range. Tosh concluded that Banting had "saved his life".

Does Gear's dilemma – increased weight gain despite efforts to eat well and train hard – sound familiar? It has become normal for us to gain weight and struggle with exercise the older we get. There is a massive disconnect between our effort and our results. We are crippled by obesity, diabetes and other ailments – considered lifestyle diseases.

GETTING BACK TO BASICS

The way of eating Gear adopted to transform his body and athletic ability is nothing new. It's how our ancestors ate to thrive and survive conditions far harsher than any we experience today. They were leaner and healthier than we are now. As a result, diseases like diabetes were not even a blip on the nutritional radar.

Roughly 195 000 years ago the planet was in the grip of a terrible Ice Age. Yet according to Prof Curtis Marean from Arizona State University in the US, the tip of the Southern Cape around Mossel Bay was one of the few places humans could survive. Recent discoveries have shown that Mossel Bay man was pretty healthy. After a bit of fishing, mollusk scavenging, the odd bit of game meat and tubers, his body formed the blueprint for what each of us sports today on day one. So what happened?

As Noakes describes in greater detail on pgs 260-268, there were three great catastrophes that occured in our nutritional evolution. Unsurprisingly, they were a result of mankind's own interference into what already worked. Dressed as progress, these three factors were to combine to form the sneaky Carbageddon pandemic that we are faced with today.

The first setback, strange though it may sound, was the advent of agriculture. As early humans moved up from Southern Africa into Europe in search of new land, we developed, transforming from hunter gatherers into pastoralists, picking up skills like the domestication of animals and learning how to harvest crops. Why wander the plains when you could raise crops, harvest grain, keep a few goats, trade grain, drink beer, get fat and start all over again? So we can't really begrudge our ancestors their pursuit of an easier life. However, if you add a couple of thousand years of innovation to "practicing" agriculture, we were bound to get too clever for our own good. Unfortunately, humans got so good at refining the agricultural process, that refined processed foodstuffs are the result today. Take a look around your supermarket outside of the fresh food aisles for anything that hasn't been processed.

The second blow happened with the passing in 1977 of the United States Dietary Goals for Americans (USDGA) based on a high-carb, low-fat diet. Unchallenged, it was to become the dietary blueprint for much of the developed world. And we've been feeling the effects – from obesity to diabetes and cancer – ever since.

The third factor was the invention of genetically modified foods. or Frankenfood, which has resulted in fruit and vegetables with much higher sugar and carbohydrate contents than the original fruit found in nature.

So here we are. Overweight. Stuck in our chairs. Waddling through life. We're desperate to be fit, slim and trim, yet held back by the very diets and medically prescribed eating plans we hope will help us change.

Bad things happen in threes or so the saying goes, so our luck, perhaps with the application of some clear-thinking science, is about to turn. Through the personal experience and clinical insight of Noakes, an award-winning scientist and one of the world's foremost experts on exercise science, as well as the professional insight of nutritionist Sally-Ann Creed and the culinary contributions of two LCHF flavour-obsessed chefs Jonno Proudfoot and David Grier, The Real Meal Revolution and its LCHF approach will change your life.

THE RENAISSANCE MAN

While our primitive ancestors may have inadvertently cracked the diet code thousands of years ago, they weren't big on documenting their daily lives, so the mantle of originator of the LCHF movement goes to William Banting circa 1862. A popular London undertaker, Banting was morbidly obese. When he started losing his hearing, his doctor, William Harvey, found that his weight was putting pressure on his ear drums. Harvey had come to the conclusion that farinaceous foods (grains, breads etc) were behind Banting's excessive weight and prescribed him a low-carb, high-fat diet. The effect of the diet on Banting's health was drastic, nothing short of miraculous in fact, and after he published his now-famous *Letter on Corpulence*, documenting his weight struggles and subsequent turnaround, the "Banting diet" and variations thereof were adopted as an effective weight-loss solution by the medical fraternity in both Europe and the USA. For the purposes of this book and because it's easier on the ear than LCHF, we will refer to LCHF as Banting in honour of the good undertaker's brave undertaking.

Fat, cooked well, is delicious. Yet through conditioning we feel guilty reaching for bacon or the fat on a nice lamb chop and try to condition ourselves not to want it. Decades of health magazines telling us it's not good for us hasn't helped, but the most serious damage to fat's reputation came from somewhere else...

THE CARBFATHER

If 1862 had been a good year for Banting and a great year for fat, 1977 was the annus horribilis for our most maligned macronutrient. In 1953, a well-respected American biochemist, Ancel Keys, published a study that erroneously highlighted fat's effect on cholesterol levels as being behind the risk of heart attack. Keys' theory, which Noakes dubs the "plumbing model" of heart disease, argued that there was a relationship between the amount of fat in the diet and heart disease. His simplistic approach concluded that by raising blood cholesterol, fat in our diet clogs our arteries and leads to heart disease, among other things.

Keys' study was deeply flawed on several counts, from his selective use of the data he had at his disposal (he omitted information from 16 of the 22 countries in the study, using only the six countries that suited his hypothesis) to the fact that his research was based solely on observational studies and not randomised clinical trials. Glaringly, he also omitted to factor in the huge growth in cigarette consumption and other variables as a possible explanation for the rise in heart disease.

Regardless of the weaknesses around the study, in 1977 Senator George McGovern and his Senate Select Committee on Nutrition and Human Needs went ahead and based their Dietary Goals for Americans (USDGA) on Keys' recommendation of a high-carb, low-fat (HCLF) diet.

It was a decision that affected us all. Ever since then, fat has been trying to rework its public image.

For more detail, turn to page 261

FAT IS YOUR FRIEND

Give us this day, our daily bacon...

... If history is written by the victors, then carbs have a significant lead. It's time to rebalance the books.

On one of his remarkable philanthropic long-distance runs, co-author of *The Real Meal Revolution* David Grier was hacking his way through outer Mongolia. Upon learning of the distances he had already run and how much further he had to go – a marathon a day for 98 days – local villagers insisted that Grier eat large amounts of pork fat because without it, they warned, he would never be able to carry on. Being an adventurous eater, Grier got stuck in. True to fact, having struggled up until that point, from then on Grier felt fuelled all day due to the slow release of energy, and he and his running partner went on to complete a mission no man had ever tackled.

What those rural Mongolians know is what our ancestors knew and what Banting discovered with the help of Harvey. It's also what our advanced urban society has forgotten. Fat is your friend. Fat fuels us. The body needs fat.

Does the idea of eating fat repulse you? As a victim of decades of anti-fat propaganda, it's not your fault you are prejudiced. You've been conditioned that way. Think about the negative reinforcement of anti-fat sentiment in society. "Low-fat" and "fat-free" products dominate the supermarket aisles. A phrase like "cut the fat" came to mean getting rid of the unwanted, the indulgently expensive or unnecessary. What did we get in return? "The best thing since sliced bread."

The consequences are grave. Due to the reinforcement of the LFHC advocacy of Keys over three decades ago and millennia of creeping carbs through agriculture and the quest for convenience of the industrial revolution, most of us still believe that eating fat is bad for you. It's also a belief that crucially we mistakenly connect with being fat, whereas (and here's the difficult part to get your head around) fat does not make you fat. Carbs do.

The focus of *The Real Meal Revolution* is to deconstruct the bad fat myth and return us to the attitude of ancient times where fat was prized.

For more on how fat fuels you and carbs that make you fat, turn to Noakes' investigations on page 258.

INSULIN - THE DEVIL WITHIN

The biggest irony of Keys' mistake is that of the three macronutrients we eat, carbohydrate is the only one that is non-essential for survival, while fat is the body's preferred fuel.

Yes, you read that right. Fat is the body's preferred fuel. Carbs are unnecessary. Cut it out and stick it to your forehead, your fridge or your wallet.

The only carbs our Pinnacle Point ancestors ate would have been seriously tough tubers with a low glycaemic index that would have taken ages to chew into submission.

Because of our genetic make-up, the majority of us are IR to some degree. So when we eat carbohydrates, our bodies react.

Here's how the insulin/carbohydrate/sugar axis of obesity works against us:

• When carbohydrates are ingested, our blood glucose levels rise.

• Insulin is secreted by the pancreas in response to the glucose entering the bloodstream from the gut. The body must be protected against sustained high blood glucose levels so the insulin causes the glucose, which is not used immediately for energy, to be stored by the liver and muscles as glycogen. Once the glycogen reserves are filled the excess glucose is stored as fat.

• If a carbohydrate cannot be removed immediately from the body (e.g. being burned off through exercise), it gets converted by the liver into fat and sent out to our fat tissues for storage. This is the body squirrelling away this energy source for a future Ice Age, only the Ice Age isn't coming. We're just getting fatter and hungrier.

The bottom line?

Insulin, your body's defence mechanism against carbs, both transforms carbs/glucose into fat and then stores it by preventing it from being used. The result? You get fat.

If you eat carbs and you don't burn a ridiculous amount of energy (even Simon Gear's nine marathons in nine weeks wasn't enough to cope with his IR levels), you will continue to get fat or maintain a consistent level of podge.

The final blow to the gut: because carbohydrates are nutrient-deficient and often packaged with salt and sugar, you feel the need to eat more of them, thereby putting yourself into a near-perpetual cycle of weight gain.

Unless, of course, you break the addiction...

HUNGER GAMES

On battlefield body, the principle anti-hunger weapon is your appestat, probably the most important body part you've never heard of.

One of the biggest stumbling blocks for people considering testing out a new way of eating is the fear of going hungry. When you go a-Banting, this won't be a problem. As Noakes goes into detail on page 270, when you move off carbs, you reconfigure your appestat, the part of your brain that regulates hunger.

When you are not Banting, you are trapped by carbs and their ability as a self-fulfilling hunger stimulant to keep you in the infinity loop of obesity. Munching on nutrient-deficient, sugar- and salt-loaded carbs makes you want more carbs, which makes you want more carbs until suddenly you're overweight and baffled by how you got there.

Hunger regulation is governed by the bulk and nutrient density of the foods we eat. The bulkier the food, the faster we feel satiated, but because bulky food – pastas, rices, bread etc – are so nutrient-deficient you will feel the need to eat sooner rather than later. Almost every food product in your local supermarket has been developed to within an inch of its life to make you eat more of it. Lost in the socio-political greed of big corporate food companies and the politicians that enable them, these edible time-bomb "foods" are designed in laboratories to be as deliciously irresistible and addictive as possible. Between the boardrooms and the laboratories of these companies, a specific junk food jargon exists. The perfect combination of salt, sugar and fat is the *bliss point*. Mouth feel is the bliss point combined with a textual factor like crunch. The *piece de resistance* for these food scientists? To achieve vanishing caloric density – where the food vanishes on your tongue so quickly you are fooled into believing you are not actually eating that much at all. So you eat more.

Now, bear in mind that carbs, the single least important macronutrient to human survival, the one with confirmed negative impacts on our bodies was the one pushed upon us in 1977 as the principle part of a healthy diet. Combine that misdirection with lax political policing of the food industry and the advanced sneakiness of massive multinational food companies and you have a recipe for disaster.

Unless of course you reconfigure and service your appestat.

In contrast to eating carbs, when you are eating fats and proteins, you will feel full for longer due to the nutrient-rich nature of these macronutrients. The added bonus is that you don't need to eat five meals a day, which if we're honest, in the hectic schedule of your average modern home is a pain to organise. When you eat fat, you simply don't get hungry in the same way carbs make you HUNGRY. The reason for this is that your appestat is functioning optimally. If you do just one thing with this book, just one life experiment, try Banting and after one week take note of what happens. You will notice the constant all-consuming hunger that usually preoccupies your mind most of the day ceases to bother you with your new Banting-processing body. And the great thing about this transformation is that you make calmer, more rational decisions when you do want to eat because it's your brain not your hunger driving you. That means fewer moments of ill-considered weakness.

WHAT TO EXPECT... WHEN YOUR BODY IS EXPECTING CARBS

The first week of your carb-free life will be tough. You might dream of sandwiches; have nightmares involving mashed potato or risotto monsters. You will experience cravings. But forewarned is forearmed. Knowing that your body is addicted to carbs, the veil had been lifted from your eyes and you are ready to take charge of your own weight, your own health.

Although some people feel instantly better, you might feel bloated and uncomfortable for a couple of days to a week. The sixth or seventh day is the toughest (they usually fall on a Saturday and Sunday because Monday is traditionally the turn-over-a-new-leaf day). You'll feel irritable and tense; you might get headaches or feel light-headed. Hang in there. If your partner starts Banting with you, all the better because you will understand each other's moods. After this, you'll feel your normal self, only better. The other plus is that after about seven days you should have lost some weight. Everyone loses weight differently – some show exponential losses in the initial weeks or months but others will lose slower.

You WILL feel better and you WILL lose weight.

If you are exercising heavily, simply increase the amount of fat you eat until you reach a point where you are no longer starving. This takes time but if you listen to your body, you'll get an idea of what you need.

Remember, there is no right amount to eat. Your body will tell you. This is about your appetite and not calories.

One of the biggest mistakes you can make is to think you need to eat more fat than you can handle. You MUST NOT force-feed yourself more fat than you can handle because you think that is how it's done. Eat your fill and carry on with life.

By force-feeding yourself (with anything) you will not feel any better nor will you lose weight. Fat is the tool we use to maintain our energy levels and appetite. You will know you're not getting enough if you get hungry before lunch or need to eat more than three times a day. You will know you're eating too much if you feel nauseous or you're not losing any weight. A ball park of between 25 to 50g of carbs per day is where you should be aiming. This is net carbs (total carbs less fibre), not 50g of potato.

Think of it this way: right now you are a fat grub wriggling on a dungheap of carbs, but about to go through an incredible metamorphosis. After a week of Banting, as your weight starts to drop, your energy levels pick up and you start to feel good about yourself, you'll be well on your way to becoming a beautiful butterfly. Don't want to be a butterfly? Okay, then you can be a moth or a cricket. But damn you'll be beautiful. You get the point.

ATHLETES
DIABETES
OBESITY
PCOS
PREGNANCY
CHILDHOOD
MENOPAUSE
DIGESTIVE CONDITIONS
ALLERGIES
CANCER

Banting is not just for overweight people and diabetics – it is a good plan for everyone, for life. We can all benefit from following it. There are different ways to apply the principles, and some people do well on more carbohydrates than others. The main thrust of the programme, however, is limiting carbohydrates while eliminating both sugar and toxic seed oils.

WHILE BANTING YOU CAN EXPECT TO HAVE:
• More energy
• Fewer (or no) cravings
• No hunger
• Weight loss
• Much better health in every aspect
• Better blood glucose and insulin readings
• Enhanced athletic performance
• Increased mental focus
• Better sleeping habits
The list of benefits is extensive, but these are the most universally experienced.

Ours is a society built on constant eating – however when Banting, snacking becomes a thing of the past. It is not unusual to find you are only eating one or two meals a day, yet without hunger between meals. Essentially you are looking to eat only when hungry and stop when you feel full. When you begin, you will probably need a week or two for the body to adapt – but once "carbohydrate adapted", hunger and cravings disappear and the need for snacks is no longer an issue. Type-1 diabetics on insulin may need to carry snacks in case of possible blood sugar lows, which is a different thing altogether. However we have yet to see a Banting diabetic who has needed to do this, even when undertaking quite rigorous exercise.

In a nutshell, Banting comprises mainly animal protein (including poultry, eggs and fish), saturated animal fats (including lard, duck fat and butter), coconut oil, olive oil and macadamia oil, some cheeses and dairy products, some nuts and seeds (if appropriate), fresh vegetables grown mostly above the ground and a few berries. There are no grains, seed oils or sugars. (See the Green, Orange and Red lists for more guidance.)

The following basics apply to everyone in virtually every stage of one's life, and will lay the foundation for the various states that follow. So it is imperative if you want to get the most out of Banting that you follow these guidelines:

• Avoid all processed food, pre-packed, boxed, fast food, food in wrappers etc.

• Exclude all sugar, fructose, maltose, agave products – anything sugary.

• Eliminate all grain products (grains are what flours are usually made of such as wheat, barley, spelt, oats, rye, corn etc) – this applies to the grain in its wholegrain form as well as its refined flour form.

• Replace all seed oils (canola, sunflower, safflower, cottonseed, grapeseed) and other inflammatory polyunsaturated oils (whether cold-pressed, extra-virgin or organic) with healthy saturated fats as outlined in this book, and be aware that 99% of prepared products will contain these damaged oils. Extra-virgin olive oil and virgin coconut oil are encouraged freely.

• Eliminate all refined carbohydrates, and if you wish to follow Banting where a few carbs are included, aim for those sourced from vegetables, not grains or sugars. If you find this difficult to begin with, aim for a little rye or oats, or perhaps some quinoa or buckwheat - but keep these to a minimum as you transition to the no-grain stage. This is important.

• If you are not intolerant to dairy products and find they do not affect your weight loss or blood sugar levels, aim for high-fat dairy products, not skim or reduced fat, light or fat-free alternatives – they must be full-fat.

• Avoid all soya products with the exception of a little MSG-free soy sauce now and then. Soya is a genetically-modified, toxic non-food with a host of problems and should not be consumed.

• A cup of home-made broth would be very helpful in terms of extra minerals needed to alleviate cramping while supplying beneficial nutrients and quality liquid to the daily diet.

UNDERCOVER BANTING

Until we get everyone else to Bant with us, there will be social occasions where you are faced with difficult decisions. Get smart, get sneaky but don't slip up.

There is always going to be the odd celebration where it's going to be impossible to dodge that piece of cheesecake, glass of sherry or lovingly made "especially for you" pasta Alfredo. Nothing offends like someone who doesn't like your food. But this is where you need to muster up all the willpower you have to indulge in a very small portion (and make sure it's taken after a protein-rich and/or fat-rich meal/snack to buffer any sugar rush). Where you can avoid having it, of course, is first prize. A great way to hide what you are eating is to take a teeny bit, and pile your plate with the salad or vegetables on offer. This gives the illusion of having a decent-sized plate of food, but in fact you have a very small amount of the "offending" food, and loads of leafy greens with a wonderful olive oil splashed over the salad. Don't forget the protein.

"SPECIAL" BANTING

Having established the fundamentals, there are different conditions and phases of life that may require tweaking of the basics to enhance the effect. We've run through all the troubleshooting for whatever your specific requirements are.

BUT AREN'T CARBOHYDRATES ESSENTIAL FOR ATHLETIC PERFORMANCE?
HOW CAN ATHLETES PERFORM TO THEIR BEST ON A LOW-CARBOHYDRATE DIET?

This is probably the question most frequently asked about Banting, especially by athletes who believe that carbohydrates are the key fuel for exercise performance. As always it is important to begin by considering the history of how we came to our current beliefs.

Until the early 1960s, athletes in Europe generally believed that eating a diet with a higher protein (meat) content was beneficial since this was the diet favoured by those who could afford to eat whatever they chose. Jim Peters, world marathon record holder in the early 1950s, one of the hardest training athletes of the era whose philosophy was to "train little, hard and often" and who performed most of his training at close to his race pace of 3min18sec/km, described how his nutrition was affected by the food shortage present when he competed in the Olympic Games: "[Before the 1952 Olympic Games], we were still rationed for meat and none extra could be obtained. At the time of the 1948 Olympics, we were given extra meat and also received food parcels from overseas. The only thing that could be done was to try make it up with extra bread and potatoes – which is probably not the best food on which to run over 100 miles a week, in training, with the extra 20 miles or so thrown in quite frequently in competition."

Clearly one of the world's most celebrated distance runners of the 1950s believed that protein and fat (meat), not carbohydrates (bread and potatoes), should be the key ingredient in the athlete's diet.

Australian Ron Clarke, set 18 world track records in the 1960s. When asked if he had ever specifically eaten a high-carbohydrate diet to improve his performance; his answer was "No". South African Jackie Mekler, five-times Comrades Marathon winner and former world record holder at ultra-marathon distances, who retired from competitive running in 1969, confirmed that athletes of that era believed that protein and fat, not carbohydrates, were the energy fuels for athletic competition.

All this changed in the mid-1960s with the development of a novel technique that allowed the muscle content of carbohydrate (glycogen) to be measured for the first time. Early researchers showed that a high-carbohydrate diet increased muscle glycogen content, a fact that is incontestable. But, as often happens in science, their subsequent finding purportedly showing that exercise performance was determined uniquely by the muscle glycogen content (and hence the amount of carbohydrates eaten in the 24 to 48 hours before the exercise bout) was accepted too rapidly and too uncritically by the scientific community. A re-analysis of that early work suggests that the findings were not as obvious as the authors wished us to believe.

The effect of these studies on athletic nutrition was electric. Within a few years, every athlete in the world "knew" that the most important determinant of athletic performance was the carbohydrate content of the diet. And so athletes were encouraged to eat diets, 75% of the energy content of which came from carbohydrates. This might mean eating 1 000g of carbohydrates a day for a cyclist in the Tour de France.

Today we need to relook those beliefs in light of the following evidence:

1. The early studies of carbohydrate loading were not performed properly because they did not include adequate control groups. They did not control for the fact that the athletes knew when they were eating the high-carbohydrate diet. This could have influenced their performances as a result of a placebo effect. We now know that the placebo effect in nutritional studies is very large. Indeed only one placebo-controlled study of carbohydrate loading has ever been performed. That study found that carbohydrate loading provided no benefit to the performance of cyclists in a 100km laboratory time trial. But because none of us believed that result we simply ignored it and continued to preach the religion of high-carbohydrate diets for athletes.

2. We now know that humans do not need carbohydrates to survive. Which does not mean that they do not provide energy during exercise and might be helpful for some athletes; the point is merely that it is entirely possible for humans to live and exercise without ever eating a single gram of carbohydrate – as have the Inuit and some other populations for thousands of years.

3. Carbohydrate in the form of glucose provides fuel for muscle contraction and for the functioning of the brain and certain other organs including the red blood cells. But the glucose for those functions can quite adequately be provided by the actions of the human liver; it does not need to be ingested.

4. Any ingested carbohydrate that is not used as energy or stored as liver or muscle glycogen must be stored as fat. This means that the carbohydrates present in a high-carbohydrate diet can only serve two functions – used as a fuel or stored as fat or glycogen. Which raises that possibility that a diet too high in carbohydrates may be deficient in protein and fat, the two macronutrients without which we cannot live. Hence it becomes increasingly likely that living on a high-carbohydrate diet might induce nutritional deficiencies. The remarkable response of athletes like Simon Gear and his father, both of whom increased their running performances when they switched from an HCLF diet to Banting, raises the possibility that their habitual HCLF was nutritionally deficient.

5. Persons with IR are unable to metabolise carbohydrates normally. Indeed those with T1DM do not increase their muscle glycogen content when they eat high-carbohydrate diets and the same may well apply to those with T2DM or lesser degrees of IR. Instead those with IR must store any excess carbohydrate as fat. This, to me, is the most likely explanation for the remarkable paradox – fat athletes who train very hard but are unable to lose any weight. The logical conclusion is that their carbohydrate intake is too high for their degree of IR (Figure 1).

6. Human performance cannot be reduced to a single variable such as the carbohydrate content of the diet and the extent to which the muscle glycogen stores are filled before exercise. Instead the effects of our nutritional choices on everything that could contribute to our performance must be considered. For example, what if a high-carbohydrate diet impairs our immune function, making us more prone to infections? Would that not be an important consideration in deciding whether or not a high-carbohydrate diet is the only option for athletes? The point is we do not yet know what all the consequences are, some of which may be unintended and potentially harmful to our performance, of eating a high-carbohydrate diet.

7. Thirty-two of the 127 respondents included in my study of the responses to the "Noakes diet" spontaneously reported that their exercise performance improved when Banting. In fact, most persons who respond well to Banting report that their energy levels increase when they cut the carbohydrates. This is clearly the opposite of the expected response if "sugar (and other carbohydrates) gives you go."

8. A high-carbohydrate diet usually contains a large proportion of energy from cereals and grains. But many people don't realise they are "allergic" to specific contents of cereals and grains and may harbour long-term chronic ill-health as a result of eating those foodstuffs. They may benefit from Banting, which excludes these allergenic foodstuffs.

Perhaps the practical information raised by all these points is that over the past few years we have moved from the absolute belief that a high-carbohydrate diet is essential for superior athletic performance to the realisation that this is certainly not true for everyone. Instead it is clear that a large proportion of athletes will do better by reducing their carbohydrate intake and eating more fat and protein. The natural conclusion is that athletes with more severe IR are more likely to benefit from this advice.

So what is an athlete to do? My advice is the following:

High performing athletes who are lean and who have no concerns about their athletic performance should continue to eat the diet that they prefer when performing well. For most I suspect this will be a high-carbohydrate diet.

But for those like myself and other South African athletes like Simon Gear, Bruce Fordyce, Oscar Chalupsky and Shaun Meiklejohn, all of whom became progressively fatter and less athletic as we aged, but who reversed this when we switched to Banting, the high-carbohydrate diet was clearly detrimental to our health, athletic performance and enjoyment of life.

So my suggestion is that any athlete who gains weight progressively with age or whose performances begin to decline dramatically and inexplicably over the course of a few years, needs to consider that the HCLF diet is the cause. The obvious suggestion is to change to Banting and see what happens. Bruce Fordyce noticed that within a week of changing to Banting, his running time in a five-kay time trial improved noticeably. Mine took somewhat longer – within six weeks I was running almost as well as I had 20 years earlier. The point is that if your running performance is going to improve while Banting, you will notice the results quite quickly. If nothing happens, then it is easy to revert to one's habitual diet.

In summary I believe that there is little reason to ingest more than 200g/day of carbohydrates regardless of how much exercise one is performing. The key is to discover the grams of carbohydrate/day that optimises one's health and performance and this will generally lie between 25 and 200g/day, the lower values for those with the most extreme IR (Figure 1).

Ingesting carbohydrates during exercise is less damaging than during rest so if one is anxious, continue ingesting carbohydrates during exercise. But those with IR probably do not need to, as IR is associated with elevated blood glucose concentrations during exercise.

THE CARDINAL SIN

Possibly the biggest error you could make with this book and Banting is to pick and choose what you want to adopt and what you want to ignore. If you choose the great part about the Banting lifestyle – the eating of fat, the wholesale embrace of delicious bacon and our advocacy for other high-fat foods like cream – but continue to eat carbs like there's a two-for-one-sale at McBurger's Fast Food, you are going to balloon. **Adopt Banting but do it properly to see results.** Sitting on the fence, dipping your toe into Banting and back into HCLF eating will result in you falling off the very fence you are sitting on. We're talking Humpty Dumpty-scale disaster. But if you adopt Banting and truly stick with the advice on the following pages, you will drop weight, feel great, still eat truly delicious food and never be harassed by constant hunger.

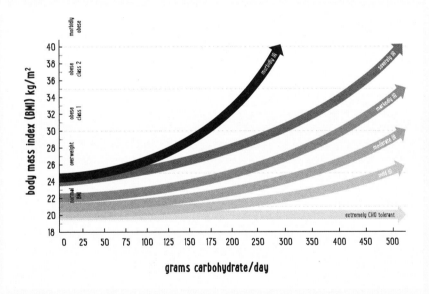

FIGURE 1: A concept figure showing the postulated relationship between the amount of carbohydrates eaten each day and the body mass index (BMI) in individuals with different degrees of insulin resistance (IR). Note that those with increasing IR have higher BMI at any given level of daily carbohydrate intake so those who are morbidly insulin resistant must cut their daily carbohydrate intakes to about 25-50g/day if they are ever to maintain a BMI less than 25kg/m².

DIABETICS

Before the discovery of insulin by Banting, Best, Macleod and Collip at the University of Toronto in 1922, children with T1DM were treated on a high-fat, extremely low calorie, low-carbohydrate diet. This prolonged survival but did not cure the disease since without insulin, the patient with T1DM will succumb to a fatal ketoacidosis.

Physicians of the day were only too happy that insulin now provided a life-saving option for the treatment of T1DM. They naturally assumed that insulin would also normalise the lives of patients with diabetes, allowing them to live to a normal age. They had yet to appreciate that the life expectancy of persons with either form of diabetes is determined by the quality of their blood glucose control, as reflected by their blood HbA1c concentrations (Figures 2 and 3).

Those with T2DM were also initially treated with a low-carbohydrate diet on the basis that reducing the carbohydrate load reduced the excretion of glucose in the urine, then the measure of "good" diabetic control.

Then inexplicably after 1950, the dietary advice for diabetics changed and patients with either T1DM or T2DM were advised to eat more carbohydrates, at least 130g/day and to build their diets around what became the 1977 USDGA Food Pyramid. The logic for this change was likely that persons with diabetes are at especially high risk for developing arterial damage and heart disease, so they must control their blood cholesterol concentrations by eating an HCLF diet.

But this is not logical for a number of reasons. First, it is their high blood glucose concentrations (Figures 2 and 3), not their normal blood "cholesterol" concentrations that cause arterial damage in both T1 and T2DM. Thus rigorous control of blood glucose concentrations around the clock is much more important.

Secondly, the key problem in both forms of diabetes is that the liver overproduces glucose in response to stimulation by a range of hormones and other stimulators that are normally held in check by a normal insulin secretion in those who are insulin sensitive and who do not have diabetes. Since persons with either form of diabetes do not have a normal insulin secretion and because those with T2DM also have IR that standard medications cannot reverse, the only logical treatment is to limit the amount of carbohydrates coming to the liver and in this way to make the control of blood glucose concentrations much easier.

Fourteen persons with T2DM informed me that they were "cured" of their diabetes when they adopted Banting and followed the "Noakes diet".

Thus the conclusion is that the best option for those with either form of diabetes is to stick to a diet that includes about 25g carbohydrates/day, which is the choice that I, as someone with T2DM, follow.

In the words of one of my colleagues to his diabetic patients: "Carbohydrates drive up your blood glucose concentration. Insulin brings your blood glucose concentration down. I can give you insulin, or you can cut your carbohydrate intake."

I believe that within the next few years patients with either form of diabetes will be advised to drastically reduce their daily carbohydrate intake to ensure that their blood HbA1c concentrations are as close to 5% as possible. For it is only those diabetics with such low HbA1c concentrations who can expect to escape the complications of this eminently treatable condition (Figures 2 and 3).

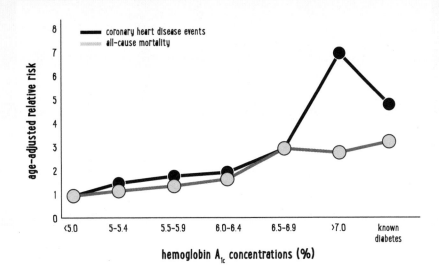

FIGURE 2: Age-adjusted relative risk of developing coronary heart disease rises as a function of the blood HbA1c concentration. Note that relative risk begins to rise steeply above an HbA1c concentration of 6.4 and is increased 7-fold in those with an HbA1c greater than 7%. This compares with an increase in relative risk of only 1.2 in those with "elevated" blood cholesterol concentrations (Table 1 on pg 283). (From Khaw et al. 2004)

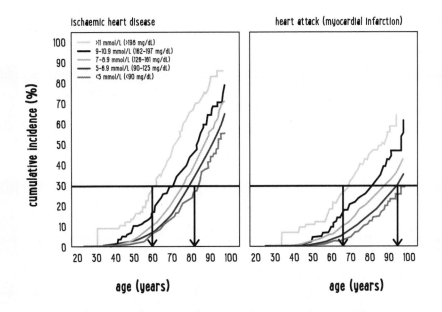

FIGURE 3: Cumulative incidence of diagnoses of ischaemic heart disease (left panel) and of heart attacks (right panel) in persons with different blood glucose concentrations measured at random. Note that risk rises at any increasing level of blood glucose concentration. The HCLF diet increases and the LCHF diet reduces random blood glucose concentrations (and HbA1c concentrations - Figure 2). (From Benn et al. 2012)

OBESITY

Obese persons can safely do this programme in exactly the same way as someone who wishes to lose five kilos. Unless there are medical complications or contra-indications that may need you to proceed cautiously, nothing will get an obese person healthier faster than eating a nutritious diet while dropping unwanted kilos. Numerous people who were previously obese report that all their health concerns were completely resolved once they lost weight in a healthy manner, cutting carbohydrates. I don't know any obese person who wouldn't want to lose weight, sleep better, take less or no medication, have perfect blood sugar readings, enjoy more energy and feel better in every way.

The question of kidney function sometimes arises. People with kidney problems may have been told to eat a reduced-protein diet, however Banting should not be viewed as high-protein, but moderate, and if tempted to overdo the protein, everyone needs to exercise restraint, not just kidney patients. Overeating is always discouraged, and when Banting, there is no need to overeat as one is easily satisfied by the extra fat content together with the adequate protein. A recent randomised controlled clinical study, which sought to evaluate weight-loss diets in people with T2DM and renal disease using differing protein amounts concluded: "Weight loss improved renal function, but differences in dietary protein had no effect." (*American Journal of Clinical Nutrition*, http://ajcn.nutrition.org/content/98/2/494.abstract)

The thing to watch out for is the diabetic on insulin or a blood sugar-lowering medication. You may find that blood sugar levels normalise rather quickly so your medication may have to be adjusted or discontinued. NB: Never discontinue or adjust medication without the guidance of a qualified health professional.

POLYCYSTIC OVARIAN SYNDROME (PCOS)

Tragically, up to 10% of all women of child-bearing age are now afflicted with this condition to some degree. PCOS manifests in several of the following ways: weight gain, mild to extremely painful and disfiguring acne, infertility, amenorrhea, painful and/or irregular menstruation, headaches, facial hair, thinning head hair and insulin resistance, as well as other distressing symptoms. While experts are not entirely sure what causes PCOS, the general consensus is that the best way to treat it is with Banting. There is always the threat of possible future diabetes if left unchecked, and often one or both parents have developed diabetes, although this is not always the case.

It makes perfect sense to use Banting to treat PCOS, as it's a classic case of insulin resistance causing the symptoms and manifestations, including raising androgens and suppressing oestrogen, both of which often revert to normal after some time Banting. But results are sometimes a little slower for some than others, and may take several months to see improvement. Nevertheless it is the only successful way to beat this often debilitating condition, and it is to be encouraged. Where Banting is too slow a process, the ketogenic diet assists in sorting out many of the symptoms a lot faster for those willing to go below 30g carbs a day. The trick is to remember to include enough fat – low-carbs and low-fat don't work.

For many couples, PCOS spells heartbreak as infertility is one of the main features of this condition. Miraculously though, many women have fallen pregnant after following Banting principles – probably due to the extra fat content. Because most women gain weight due to insulin resistance with PCOS, their natural instinct is to eat very low-fat – thanks to the bad science taught about fat – and this only compounds the problem. Imagine their delight when they increase fat intake, lose weight and find they are expecting the baby they never thought they would have!

PREGNANCY

Bearing in mind that this is a healthy lifestyle, there is absolutely no risk to either mother or child from healthy eating. Studies on pregnant women are unethical so no documented studies with control groups exist to "prove" low-carb pregnancies are better than high-carb ones, but it certainly makes a lot of sense so long as there is sufficient fluid and caloric intake from protein, healthy fats and nutritious vegetables. Avoiding processed food becomes even more important when pregnant.

Low-carb eating during pregnancy also protects against the risk of high blood pressure and gestational diabetes, which seems to be on the increase with the surfeit of junk food available. Poor maternal diet may predispose the unborn child to metabolic syndrome later in life, as well as possible heart disease, diabetes, various cancers and obesity. Mum's diet will affect that child for the rest of his or her life. And while ketosis is not recommended specifically, it probably wouldn't harm the baby as many mums unintentionally spend a large amount of time in their first trimester in ketosis due to nausea and the inability to eat.

HELPFUL GUIDELINES FOR WOMEN WHO WANT TO PURSUE A BANTING PREGNANCY:
• Increase intake of whole eggs, liver, bone marrow and other animal fats – your baby's brain development depends on high-quality fat.
• Include fatty fish without fear.
• Limit fruit to two portions a day but avoid extremely sweet fruits like grapes. If you are struggling with sugar or weight issues, exclude fruit.
• If nauseous, try eating fat later in the day as part of a fatty cut of meat, rather than a fatty breakfast. Nausea usually abates after 12 weeks, but a P-5-P form of vitamin B6 is also helpful in eliminating nausea.

PARTICULARLY GOOD FOOD TO EAT DURING PREGNANCY INCLUDES:

LIVER
A nutrient-dense, protein-rich food – eat two to three times a week for the pre-formed vitamin A (retinol), iron, B12, zinc and folate (the naturally-occurring form of folic acid) – all vital for the growing foetus.

MEAT, FISH, CHICKEN, EGGS, OFFAL, GAME, DUCK
These provide much-needed protein in high-quality bioavailable form. Only animal products contain heme iron, the most easily assimilated form of iron. If you are limiting or avoiding grains, you have removed the iron-inhibiting phytates found in grains. Phytates are plant salts that block the absorption of iron, zinc and calcium, so they can play a major role in preventing uptake of vital nutrients for mother and child. Make sure to eat around 10 to 20% animal protein as this is a moderate protein plan; large amounts are not required. Don't leave out the fat though, your milk quality depends on it. It's no surprise in terms of calories that 55% of breast milk is fat, 38% carbs and 7% protein.

FISH
Particularly fatty fish, which is high in the long-chain omega-3 essential fatty acids eicosapentaenoic acid (EPA) and docosahexaenoic acid (DHA). These fats are needed to build the baby's brain and eyes in utero as well as in the first two years of infancy. Research also shows a connection between EPA and DHA and a reduction in the amount of cases of post-partum depression. Choose fatty fish with teeth like mackerel, salmon and herring, and very fatty small fish such as sardines and anchovies. Don't fear eating fish while pregnant due to mercury levels. Fish is abundant in selenium, a natural protection against any mercury present – therefore eating fish with mercury is not a concern as the level of selenium is (in almost all cases) higher than the level of mercury, making it safe to eat.

Selenium binds to mercury, preventing it from binding to anything else such as brain tissue, and it's then excreted – a natural chelating agent if you like. These rules apply to fish whether it is raw or cooked. Cooking does nothing to change mercury levels. Avoid fish such as shark, swordfish, king mackerel and tilefish due to higher than normal levels of mercury.

Mum's gut flora is also of prime importance in influencing the immunity of the foetus in utero. Eat kefir, sauerkraut and fermented foods, which support beneficial bacteria in the human digestive system. Incidentally, as the baby passes through the birth canal, it will pick up the "fingerprint" of mum's gut flora – a powerful reason to not be hoodwinked into having a C-section (C-section babies have sterile guts), and of course to make sure your gut flora is optimal for the length of the pregnancy and feeding phases and thus pass on a "legacy" of beneficial bacteria to your baby.

CHILDHOOD

On 17 March 2005, the *New York Times* reported on a paper from the *New England Journal of Medicine* stating that this would be the first generation of children whose life expectancy would be shortened by obesity, and that the severity of the obesity epidemic would produce earlier onset of all the major diseases previously only seen in old age. They are expected to die much earlier than their parents.

We have become so used to seeing overweight children now that children of normal weight or even a bit on the skinny side are deemed to be unhealthy. Fifty years ago obesity in children was almost unheard of. As more and more meals are based on or bulked up with starchy breads, rice, pasta and potatoes, one in three children are now obese, and the number is growing. The prevalence of children under 10 years old with T2DM, which used to be called "late-onset" diabetes, is also tragically on the increase – in childhood! These children are both diabetic and very overweight – a condition someone has aptly coined "diabesity". Something is very wrong.

Obese and overweight children almost always go on to become overweight adults. Training children to avoid pastries, sweets, processed food, fizzy drinks and take-away food sounds like a no-brainer, but this is often viewed as "deprivation" by society. By restricting carbs in childhood, you are offering them the gift of a long, healthy life, not deprivation. To appreciate the alternative, one just has to look around and realise how many people are sick and overweight; radiant health is no longer the norm. Feeding a child a low-carbohydrate diet will not only improve mental aptitude and focus, but prevent serious health hazards later on.

One of the best recognised and highly recommended treatments for autism and epilepsy is, in fact, a ketogenic diet. The well-known ketogenic diet is an eating plan where all carbohydrate foods (including fruit and carb-rich foods) are removed from the child's diet, and he/she is placed on a very high-fat diet, together with sufficient protein and vegetables. The body is therefore forced to burn fats instead of carbohydrates. Carbs are turned into glucose, particularly important for brain function. Where there are no carbohydrates provided, the liver then converts fat into ketone bodies. These can then be used by the brain as a source of energy, and has been shown to lead to a dramatic decline in seizure occurrence in epileptic children. The ketogenic diet has been successfully used for decades, so clearly it is neither dangerous nor unhealthy. However, feeding a moderate carbohydrate diet that includes sweet potato, carrots, nuts and even a little gluten-free grain in moderation (such as buckwheat and quinoa) in small amounts and infrequently – would be acceptable for most healthy children.

Breakfast cereals may just be the elephant in the room. Many parents can't imagine giving children anything else to eat at breakfast other than a plate of cereal, with reduced-fat milk, plenty of sugar and perhaps a glass of orange juice and a piece of toast with margarine. This is a recipe for disaster for the rest of the day, as there is virtually no protein or fat. The fat that is provided is a toxic version of a real fat. Margarine is no substitute for butter whatsoever – one is toxic and inflammatory, the other (butter) is nutritious and healthy. You may as well open a packet of sugar and pour this down the child's throat. It is no wonder there are so many "diagnoses" of Attention Deficit Hyperactivity Disorder (ADHD). Remedial teachers wouldn't have had a job 60 years ago as it didn't exist, but today there are not enough teachers to go around.

On the subject of ADHD, the man who "invented" it, US psychiatrist Leon Eisenberg, recognised as the "scientific father of ADHD", said in his final interview at the age of 87: "ADHD is a prime example of a fictitious disease". At the end of the day, withdrawing excess carbohydrates and sugar from the diet would effectively remove this "condition" almost entirely, no drugs required.

To summarise, for the normal child, don't take all carbs away, but make sure the carbs given are not in the form of grains or sugars – and before going to parties, fill them up with fat and protein. They will eat a lot less junk.

MENOPAUSE

Menopause is a great opportunity to implement Banting as it's a time when a woman usually discovers her adrenal function is low, and only Banting really makes a difference to the symptoms. It's a time of life where many women find they have little or no energy, their emotions are all over the place, bones are not that good anymore and she has an ever-widening waistline. It also seems that what she gains in weight around the middle, she loses in the memory department. Far too many women suffer needlessly without realising the valuable role the right food can play in improving how they feel, and drugs don't have to be a first option. A study presented at the Endocrine Society's 95th Annual Meeting in San Francisco on 17 July 2013 found that overweight women who lost weight increased activity in the areas of the brain responsible for memory tasks; there seems to be a strong correlation between belly fat and cognitive decline in everyone in fact, not just menopausal women.

Good adrenal function is rare in women of menopausal age due to the traumas and joys of bringing up children, on-the-run high-carb diets, and all the things life throws at a wife and mother in her 50s when menopause typically occurs. Women who have maintained their weight, exercised and have followed a healthy diet for a significant length of time do best when they go into menopause, but for the rest, it can be very challenging.

The adrenal glands are two little walnut-sized glands that sit on top of each kidney like little hats. They have been called the Napoleons of the body due to the power they wield over emotions, stamina and the production of essential hormones after menopause. Banting is critical for supporting adrenal function. Carbohydrates seriously undermine adrenal function, yet these are the "comfort foods" many will turn to, exacerbating the problem.

By eliminating carbohydrates, the insulin resistance common to most women at this age can be reversed, the spare tyre disappears and their memory miraculously returns (well, most of it anyway). When adrenal function is low, various allergies surface together with skin rashes, mood swings, headaches, respiratory problems, exhaustion, hot flushes and insomnia, however many women report a lessening or complete disappearance of almost all these conditions when they follow Banting.

DIGESTIVE CONDITIONS

GUT FLORA

We have roughly 500 identified strains of bacteria in our digestive tracts, and more "bugs" than cells in our bodies – over three trillion in fact. These are crucial to healthy digestive function. Without enough healthy bacteria in our digestive tracts, immunity and general health is severely impaired. A high-carb diet together with stress, environmental pollutants, medications, antibiotics and infections can kill off significant colonies of bacteria, leaving the host vulnerable to yeasts and pathogens that feed on high-carbohydrate foods, and their by-products and waste cause untold misery to the host.

Carbohydrates in excess are particularly destructive where gut flora are concerned. Restricting carbohydrates without restoring the ecology of the digestive tract with probiotic foods doesn't make sense as it could take many years to return the colon to health without them. They are fragile and while many are resident bacteria, others are transient and need to be replenished regularly.

Although they have saved countless lives, antibiotics have become an enemy of health in many ways. Today, more antibiotics are used to fatten livestock globally than are taken by human beings for infectious conditions, creating the antibiotic resistance we see sweeping the world. Plus, antibiotics appear in the water supply, sprayed on vegetables and added to animal feed. While these drugs fatten livestock, they cause antibiotic resistance in humans. A short course is no longer enough in many people – two to three courses are required, and in taking these drugs, valuable bowel flora are destroyed. Meat and poultry not pasture-fed without antibiotics have compromised flora and the quality of the meat is severely lacking in nutrition. The drugs are passed on to us, compromising our flora as well. For this reason, fermented foods like kefir, kimchi and sauerkraut are invaluable, and used to be a very important part of everyone's diet 50 to 100 years ago.

Fermented foods fell from favour with the advent of modern processed food, and had almost disappeared until organisations like Weston Price began to encourage the reintroduction of such foods into our diets, which greatly help to reconstitute depleted flora. Fortunately Sally Fallon Morrell published a timeless handbook on this subject, *Nourishing Traditions*, for anyone wanting to resurrect these ancient culinary skills.

DIGESTIVE COMPLAINTS

These are usually the first disorders to resolve when Banting, and relatively rapidly too. Gas, bloating, oesophageal reflux (sometimes called GERD or GORD), heartburn, a feeling of fullness for many hours, gallstones, and even diverticulitis, Crohn's Disease, irritable bowel syndrome (IBS) and other maladies of the digestive system seem to abate quickly when Banting.

On a high-carbohydrate, fibre-poor diet many people feel the need to supplement fibre to keep themselves regular, however Banting provides natural vegetable fibre, which the body eventually adapts to rather than the grain-based fibres used to bring relief from digestive discomfort and constipation. In the early adaption phase of Banting, constipation can be a problem for some people so obtaining relief by supplementing psyllium husks is suggested. Psyllium provides soluble fibre from portions of the seed of the Plantago ovate plant. The benefit of taking this kind of fibre is that it draws water like a sponge, bulking up the contents for easier evacuation. As a source of soluble dietary fibre, psyllium husks often relieve constipation and maintain regular gastro-intestinal transit of food for people with sluggish systems. Taking fibre is not ideal, but it's a better bet than the bran-based kind of fibre that is damaging to the colon, and so much better than mineral oil-based laxatives, which irritate the mucous membranes of the digestive tract, compounding the problem and setting up dependency. Note that whenever more fibre is added to the diet, more water is needed. In essence though, eating more kefir, sauerkraut and even taking probiotics will ultimately go a long way to solving this problem. Soon, hopefully no extra fibre will be necessary, but psyllium is a safe interim measure while you get the health of your digestive tract back.

GALLBLADDER DISEASE

There appears to be no evidence that fats are responsible for gallbladder disease whatsoever, so having a gallbladder removed should not pose a problem for someone wishing to start Banting. People are usually told to avoid fat after gallbladder surgery, and certain people do appear to struggle with fat intake afterwards. This is usually due to low stomach acid, impaired liver function, continued poor diet or insufficient bowel flora – or all of the above. Initially if you struggle with fats after gallbladder removal, use a digestive enzyme blend containing lipase (a fat-digesting enzyme) and together with the fibrous vegetables you should experience relief. By cutting carbs your symptoms should improve, while only cutting fats will not have the same effect. Eventually your body will adjust and none of these will be necessary.

CANDIDA

Because a high-carbohydrate diet is loaded with sugar in the form of bread, potatoes, simple sugars and processed food, the yeast candida albicans can grow freely in the digestive tract – at times getting so out of control as to become systemic, causing serious illness – even cancer. The beauty of Banting is that all sugary foods are eliminated, making this the perfect anti-candida diet. Of course it's a good idea to supplement with probiotics to ensure that the colonies of healthy bacteria are replenished to a degree where they can reduce the yeast to normal levels. We do need some of this organism as it forms part of our ecology, but not the dizzy heights carbs can raise these levels to.

HALITOSIS/BAD BREATH

Bad breath is noticeable when you first go into ketosis, and usually passes quite quickly with good oral hygiene. There are some other reasons though. When your protein levels are too high and your fat intake is too low, you may have this nasty experience. Embarking on Banting does not mean having a high-protein diet and a low-fat diet which is what happens to some people who don't get it right. Remember Banting consists of low-carbohydrates, moderate protein and higher than normal fat intake. By eating more vegetables you will be getting more chlorophyll, which is a natural deodorant, and making a daily green drink with leaves and water in a blender will definitely help the problem. A key cause is often lactose intolerance from eating dairy products. Eliminate all dairy except butter, then slowly add another type of dairy product (cheese, cream, yoghurt etc) every five or so days, and see when the dragon breath kicks in. You might do well on much less dairy or on no dairy at all – everyone is different. Self-experimentation is the easiest way to find out where you stand.

FOOD ALLERGIES/SENSITIVITIES

A food allergy would result in anaphylactic shock, and if not treated, death, whereas a food sensitivity elicits symptoms of pain, inflammation, digestive discomfort, insomnia, rashes and chronic illnesses such as sinusitis, arthritis, headaches and asthma. These usually disappear when the offending food is eliminated.

Sometimes perceived food intolerances are actually a symptom of "leaky gut syndrome", a condition where through antibiotic abuse or other medications, stress or yeast overgrowth, a part of the digestive tract develops little openings, called tight junctions, between the cells. Whole proteins can now slip through these tight junctions, into the bloodstream, to which the body reacts, gradually causing the host to become sensitive to a number of foods until the ecology of the gut is restored with Banting and beneficial flora, which helps to close the gaps. Therefore not all sensitivities are true sensitivities; a previous food intolerance may have abated if the food is reintroduced six months after starting Banting.

By Banting, you are giving your body its best chance to heal and alleviate "allergies". Banting is anti-inflammatory by nature, which allows the body to strengthen its reserves and overcome many sensitivities.

CANCER

There is mounting evidence that a ketogenic diet is a powerful alternative cancer treatment. This diet is one where carbohydrates are kept to 25g or less in order to form ketones or ketone bodies. Ketone bodies are three different chemicals formed when fatty acids are broken down by the liver for energy. Two of these are good energy sources for the heart and brain, but the third (acetone) is a waste product and is excreted via the lungs, and may manifest as halitosis. A state of ketosis is reached when ketones are formed in the body through withdrawal of carbohydrates. These ketones are molecules generated during fat metabolism, and are a sign that your body is now using fat for energy. In the absence of ketones, the body will burn available glucose and fat will not be burned, so this process forces the body to burn fat.

It is important to distinguish between ketosis and type-1 diabetic ketoacidosis, which can be very dangerous. The normal body will avoid this by producing insulin, where the type-1 diabetic is unable to produce insulin to prevent it. Type-2 diabetics usually have enough insulin and will not enter this state. Ketosis may occur at slightly different levels for different people – anywhere from 0 to 50g of carbohydrates a day can produce ketosis, however the general consensus is that around 20 to 25g of carbs a day will do it.

In order for this process to affect cancer cells, you would replace carbohydrates with healthy fats and protein. By cutting out the "food" of cancer cells – glucose and fructose – you cut off their life-support and force them to die. When cells are deprived of this fuel, they will have to resort to using fat-based ketones. Normal cells can switch between glucose and ketone bodies, but cancer cells lack that flexibility.

All the food eaten would be natural, whole food that is very low-carb, such as animal protein, saturated fat, olive oil, avocado, above the ground vegetables, and filtered water. There would be total avoidance of processed food, fizzy drinks, toxic oils, processed meats and any fast food.

When fighting cancer, only the best will do. Grass-fed beef, pasture-reared chickens, organic vegetables etc. Because hormones and tainted foods are fed to animals, pesticides sprayed on vegetables and genetically modified soya and corn is routinely fed to chickens and livestock, one has to be committed to quality in order to avoid the hazards of these other substances, highly carcinogenic in themselves.

Dr Dominic Agostino and researchers from the University of South Florida Medical School are among the pioneers in this field.

As you start Banting, you will need to:

• Toss out the offending foods and non-foods.

• Decide on what you would like to eat while Banting.

• Shop for the correct ingredients – have a look at the recipes and use as many of these as possible to make this a super-tasty experience. The recipes are all carefully designed to fit into Banting so using this book is safe in every aspect.

• Start with your fridge. Is there anything that will tempt you to go off the rails? Clean out the fridge and ready it for the fresh produce. Don't even give yourself the chance to cheat by hiding something you like behind something healthy. Out of sight is not out of mind. You know if it is there.

• The grocery cupboard. Examine the tins of food, sauces, dressings and pasta mixes – none of these will be suitable so get rid of them. Are there boxes of cereal, chips and other treats there? All these foods have hidden carbs and sugars, and they will derail your best efforts. Do you have potatoes, crackers, pasta, rice or white flour in the cupboard? Get rid of it – it's the only way to prepare your mind and get yourself ready for your new life. Failing to plan is planning to fail.

• Shopping spree. Check out the recipes and make a shopping list. Shopping every few days for fresh ingredients full of nutrients is preferable to having vegetables lose their appeal and nutrition, which may mean you will waste food and money. While shopping always ask yourself What Would Banting Do (WWBD)? Perhaps get it made into a bangle.

• By planning ahead from the recipes you won't have any wasted ingredients. Plan a week or a few days at a time. Make more of the foods you can freeze, and on busy days you can head to the freezer for a Banting meal and just add a salad.

INDISPENSABLES

It helps to always have the following stalwart Banting staples in the fridge for quick meals and snacks if necessary:

Roast chicken – don't throw out the skin, you need that
Boiled eggs – they're good for you so help yourself
Cut-up vegetables or crudités – use these to dip into anything — patés, cream cheese...
Shaved biltong or cold meats like salami – just like that
Nuts and seeds – have a look at the Red, Orange and Green lists to see what's hot and what's not
Fresh berries – these are higher in sugar than the nuts so best follow the guidelines in the Orange list
Ripe avocados – neat, with a twist of lime, black pepper and a splash of olive oil, or as a dip
Cheese – heavenly cheese! If you're not lactose intolerant, cheese satisfies the appetite like nothing on earth. Really mature, ripe cheese also does wonders for the gut flora
Water – you need it. Drink it often

VEGETABLES

Almost all permitted carbohydrates in Banting come from vegetables. They offer an enormous range of nutrients. For example, just one cup of broccoli boasts 116mg vitamin C, 76mcg folate, 456mg potassium and 72mg calcium. And that's not including the phytochemicals, the fibre or any of the other complex nutrients – all for under five grams net carbs a cup. Cruciferous vegetables are powerful anti-carcinogens, and the leafy greens such as spinach, cabbage, Brussels sprouts and kale can all be eaten freely. They are self-limiting, nobody gets "addicted" to them, so they are regarded as "eat all you like" foods.

By steaming broccoli for just 90 seconds you will derive the most sulphoraphane and indole-3-carbinol from it – two incredibly powerful anti-cancer agents. It's advisable to steam brassica vegetables lightly as it renders the goitrogens present in these vegetables inactive. Goitrogens are responsible for depressing thyroid function in some people, so if your thyroid is under-active you don't want to eat a lot of raw broccoli, cauliflower and cabbage.

Brightly coloured vegetables are power houses of important phytochemicals, antioxidants and nutrients that support eye and brain health, mop up free radicals, provide fibre, extra liquid, delicious taste and – in the case of garlic and onions – natural antibiotics and probiotics. The fibre from plants, together with intestinal bacteria, is responsible for the production of short-chain fatty acids (SCFA) that feed the walls of the intestine and protect against intestinal cancers.

Some vegetables deliver greater benefits when they are cooked than in their raw state. While carrots are limited due to their higher carb content, a substance called falcarinol, found in carrots, has been shown to reduce the risk of cancer, according to researchers at the Danish Institute of Agricultural Sciences (DIAS). Kirsten Brandt, head of the research department, commented that isolated cancer cells grow more slowly when exposed to falcarinol, a polyacethylen.

Tomatoes are very beneficial cooked, as only in their cooked form is lycopene able to be absorbed by the body as a protective measure against prostate cancer. Lycopene is only released in the presence of fat, so be generous with the fat when sautéing them. Garlic contains sulphur, flavonoids and selenium – all potent anti-cancer agents, working mainly in the digestive tract and preventing organ cancers.

Avoiding fat when cooking onions prevents the rich source of quercetin (a powerful antioxidant and anti-histamine) from being released and absorbed. Onions are also good for normalising blood viscosity and fighting infection. They have even been credited with helping to detoxify heavy metals like cadmium and arsenic from the body, which cause cancer, due to the high levels of cysteine and methionine (amino acids) present. These amino acids are also present to a lesser extent in egg yolks. There is a fair amount of vitamin C to be found in onions, which is also known for detoxifying heavy metals.

PROTEIN

Proteins are long complex chains of amino acids, which are our body's building blocks, needed for building and repair. The body is made up almost entirely of protein excluding bone and water. The only readily available natural sources of "complete" proteins (those which contain all of the essential amino acids needed) include seafood, poultry, eggs, beef, lamb, game and dairy products. Many other foods contain some protein, but only animal protein is "complete" protein. Vegetarian protein is not complete protein, and various different food sources are needed to make up those amino acids. However, a vegetarian diet by nature is a carbohydrate rich diet, and usually a very low-fat diet. You can see the problem here for the success of this programme if vegetarian. It is a very unsuccessful way of attempting to lose weight while building muscle and attaining excellent health.

FAT

Dietary fats are essential to life and good health, and are pivotal to attaining permanent weight loss and glowing health. Some fats are not good for you, such as hydrogenated or partially hydrogenated fats (found in margarines, commercial-baked and processed foods), all seed oils and trans fats. (Trans fats are damaged fats found in many margarines, seed oils and processed food.) All these unhealthy fats are high in omega-6 fatty acids, are extremely inflammatory, and vie for position of receptor sites with the healthier omega-3 fatty acids. By taking in too many omega-6s, you sabotage the body's ability to make use of omega-3s, which are anti-inflammatory and health-promoting.

Better fats and oils to choose are those which are found in nature and are more stable, such as lard, duck fat and butter, as well as coconut oil, olive oil and macadamia nut oil. When cooking, saturated fat is superior to all other fats due to its stability. Healthy fat intake does not lead to fat storage, unless it is mixed with sugar and other carbohydrates. Fat functions well with protein and thus by avoiding high-carbohydrate-containing foods, especially if refined, you will spare yourself the inflammation that accompanies this way of eating.

CARBOHYDRATES

The reason for cutting carbohydrates is because carbohydrates elicit an insulin response. Insulin is both an inflammatory hormone and a fat-storing hormone, which we wish to keep as low as possible, using only the bare minimum to remove glucose from the bloodstream to turn it into energy. The excess is stored as fat, and this acts as a back-up fuel supply. The problem is that in today's age we aren't fleeing woolly mammoths and we seldom use up the stored fuel, and continue to eat so much in the way of carbohydrates for the body to use immediately, that the stored fat is never needed, and continues to be built upon.

By keeping the body's level of glucose in a narrow range, you prevent the huge release of insulin that is usually required to clear the glucose from the blood after a high-carbohydrate meal. Stable blood sugar allows the body to begin to burn the stored fat as energy.

WHY SOYA, CORN AND MSG ARE NOT ADVOCATED WHEN BANTING
SOY/SOYA

Soya is never recommended by anyone who has a shred of scientific nutritional knowledge. Firstly, it's a very poor source of protein and shouldn't be confused with "real" animal protein and secondly this is no alternative at all. Soybeans are a very cheap crop to grow, and over 95% is genetically modified (GMO). But even "organic" soya has toxic phytochemicals, and an extensive list of problems is associated with its use, including:

• Suppression of thyroid hormones (causing hypothyroidism and goitres)
• Digestive distress
• Some cancers
• Immune system breakdown
• Severe allergies
• ADD and ADHD
• Higher risk of heart disease
• Malnutrition (phytates present prevent absorption of protein, calcium, magnesium, iron and zinc)
• Possesses anti-nutrients: phytates, enzyme inhibitors and goitrogens
• Very high levels of oestrogen, affects sperm (Harvard study showed correlation between soy intake and low sperm count)

- Promotes fat storage
- Soybean oil linked to cancer
- Hexane is used during manufacture

CORN

Like soya, corn is virtually always GMO, and is also a very high-carbohydrate food. The carb value also rises dramatically with each stage of the refining process, from coarse to the finest flour or starch; corn comes in many forms. It is also one of those ubiquitous products which, like soya, has invaded every kind of processed food. A poor source of nutrients; we suggest you avoid corn entirely.

MONOSODIUM GLUTAMATE (MSG)

Dr Russell Blaylock, a US neurosurgeon, is one of the experts in the dangers of MSG. He says the cells of the brain literally "excite themselves to death" in the presence of MSG. It is a taste enhancer and is found as dozens of aliases, one of the most common being "textured vegetable protein". An exceptionally toxic substance, it has no place in anyone's diet – eating real food will be your best protection against MSG, as it is added to almost all processed food to improve taste.

FERMENTED FOODS

Fermenting food is a lost art – a practice used to keep the digestive and immune systems healthy, as the digestive system makes up 70% of the body's entire immune system. A healthy balance of good and bad bacteria needs to be maintained for optimal health. The gut is known as the second brain and contains more neurotransmitters than the brain itself.

Diet plays a key role in keeping the gut healthy, and fermented foods are the perfect way to replenish healthy gut bacteria as they provide the body with natural probiotics. Traditional cultures from the beginning of time have all had fermented foods, even though they may not have understood their role in the body. There were no refrigerators so fermenting food was a wonderful way to preserve food as well as provide healing properties to the body. The process enhances nutrient content with beneficial microbes and enzymes, and valuable vitamin K2 is provided to the body, which may prevent heart disease and osteoporosis.

Lacto-fermentation involves plunging vegetables into salt-water brine that kills any unwanted microbes, allowing the beneficial bacteria to proliferate. A chemical reaction then occurs causing lactobacilli to break down the starches and sugars of the vegetable and produce lactic acid, preserving the vegetables. A nutrient-dense food is created, which is highly therapeutic when eaten in small amounts, adding a few spoons to one's food daily. Fermented foods nourish, balance and help heal the gut and enhance immunity.

STEVIA, SUGAR ALCOHOLS AND ARTIFICIAL SWEETENERS

These are very helpful in the interim stage of suddenly switching from a sugary diet to a no-sugar diet. It can be extremely difficult for some people, and while the ideal is to retrain your taste buds away from the desire for sugar, realistically this is only going to be the experience of very few. If a sugar alcohol or natural sweetener such as stevia helps to avoid resorting to sugar or artificial sweeteners, it is worth using them. With their low or zero carb count, sugar alcohols can be used to bring flavour to some foods.

Stevia is a natural herb and has been shown to have blood-sugar balancing benefits, no calories, no carbs and is 600 times sweeter than sugar, so just a tiny bit of powder or liquid is used in sweetening a beverage or dish. This would be the sweetener of choice, but one could also use a sugar alcohol such as erythritol or xylitol for baking. These can mean the difference between continuing to Bant and returning to a sugary diet. They taste almost identical to sugar, but are considerably more expensive.

Artificial sweeteners (including sucralose, acusulfame K, cyclamates and saccharine) on the other hand are particularly harmful to the body and the brain, and amazingly – though being touted as "slimming aids" – have been shown to increase hunger and cause weight gain. The added benefit of sugar alcohols is that if you have too much (over nine teaspoons a day), you will have looser stools, and it may combat a troublesome constipation problem in the early stages of Banting, but that's the worst that can happen. Stevia does not have this effect, and it has been shown to help balance blood sugar.

SOME POINTS TO REMEMBER:

- Avoid excessive protein intake (the size and thickness of your palm without fingers is a good measure for a serving of animal protein).
- Choose fatty cuts of meat (often cheaper and tastier).
- Include a variety of foods. Diversity provides a wider spectrum of nutrients.
- Purchase foods you recognise in their natural state, ie. eat real food.
- Avoid processed and fast food.
- Stop eating when full, but satisfied.
- Don't be too hard on yourself but do your best to get into the diet as soon as possible.
- Plan ahead.

• FINALLY: be aware that most of what you have been taught is simply wrong. Fat is not the enemy. good quality meat is very healthy. a low-fat diet is very unhealthy. and eggs every day will not lead to heart disease – just the opposite in fact.

Banting can only work if it reduces your calorie intake by making you less hungry. If Banting fails to reduce your hunger. allowing you to eat much less frequently – every six to 12 hours instead of every three hours as typically occurs in those following the HCLF eating plan – then it will not produce the weight loss you require.

RED ORANGE AND GREEN – THE LISTS TO LIVE YOUR LIFE BY

These lists will help to make Banting easy to follow. Traffic rules apply. Green means go. Orange means proceed with caution and Red means no.

GREEN is an all-you-can-eat list – you can choose anything you like without worrying about the carbohydrate content as all the foods will be between 0 to 5g/100g.

It will be almost impossible to overdo your carbohydrate intake by sticking to this group of foods. Over eating protein is not recommended, so eat a moderate amount of animal protein at each meal. Include as much fat as you are comfortable with – bearing in mind that Banting is high in fat. Caution: even though these are all-you-can-eat foods, only eat when hungry, stop when full and do not overeat. The size and thickness of your palm without fingers is a good measure for a serving of animal protein.

ANIMAL PROTEIN (unless these have a rating, they are all 0g/100g)
All eggs
All meats, poultry and game
All natural and cured meats
(pancetta, parma ham, coppa etc)
All natural and cured sausages
(salami, chorizo etc)
All offal
All seafood (except swordfish and tilefish
– high mercury content)
Broths

DAIRY
Cottage cheese
Cream
Cream cheese
Full-cream Greek yoghurt
Full-cream milk
Hard cheeses
Soft cheeses

FATS
Any rendered animal fat
Avocado oil
Butter
Cheese – firm, natural, full-fat, aged cheeses
(not processed)
Coconut oil
Duck fat
Ghee
Lard
Macadamia oil
Mayonnaise, full fat only (not from seed oils
– see recipe for coconut mayo in "Basics")
Olive oil

FLAVOURINGS AND CONDIMENTS
All flavourings and condiments are okay, provided they do not contain sugars and preservatives or vegetable oils.

NUTS AND SEEDS
Almonds
Flaxseeds (watch out for pre-ground flaxseeds, they go rancid quickly and become toxic)
Macadamia nuts
Pecan nuts
Pine nuts
Pumpkin seeds
Sunflower seeds
Walnuts

SWEETENERS
Erythritol granules
Stevia powder
Xylitol granules

VEGETABLES
All green leafy vegetables
(spinach, cabbage, lettuces etc)
Any other vegetables grown above the ground
Artichoke hearts
Asparagus
Aubergines
Avocados
Broccoli
Brussels sprouts
Cabbage
Cauliflower
Celery
Courgettes
Leeks
Mushrooms
Olives
Onions
Peppers
Pumpkin
Radishes
Sauerkraut
Spring onions
Tomatoes

ORANGE is made up of ingredients containing between 6g and 25g of carbs per 100g (6% - 25%).

Chart your carbohydrates without getting obsessive and still obtain an excellent outcome. If you are endeavouring to go into ketosis, this list will assist you to not overshoot the 25 to 50g/100g limit. These are all net carbs and they are all 23 to 25g per indicated amount. Ingredients are all fresh unless otherwise indicated.

FRUITS
Apples 1.5
Bananas 1 small
Blackberries 3.5 C
Blueberries 1.5 C
Cherries (sweet) 1 C
Clementines 3
Figs 3 small
Gooseberries 1.5 C
Grapes (green) under 1 C
Guavas 2
Kiwi fruits 3
Litchis 18
Mangos, sliced, under 1 C
Nectarines 2
Oranges 2
Pawpaw 1
Peaches 2
Pears (Bartlett) 1
Pineapple, sliced, 1 C
Plums 4
Pomegranate ½
Prickly pears 4
Quinces 2
Raspberries 2 C
Strawberries 25
Watermelon 2 C

NUTS
Cashews, raw, 6 T
Chestnuts, raw, 1 C

SWEETENERS
Honey 1t

VEGETABLES
Butternut 1.5 C
Carrots 5
Sweet potato 0.5 C

KEY
C = cups per day
T = tablespoons per day
t = teaspoons per day
g = grams per day

For example: Apples 1.5 are all the carbs you can have for the day

RED

will contain all the foods to avoid as they will be either toxic (ie. seed oils. soya) or high-carbohydrate foods (ie. potatoes. rice). We strongly suggest you avoid all the items on this list or, at best, eat them very occasionally and restrict the amount when you do. They will do nothing to help you in your attempt to reach your goal.

BAKED GOODS/GRAIN-BASED FOODS

All flours from grains – wheat flour, cornflour, rye flour, barley flour, pea flour, rice flour etc
All forms of bread
All grains – wheat, oats, barley, rye, amaranth, quinoa, teff etc
Beans (dried)
"Breaded" or battered foods
Brans
Breakfast cereals, muesli, granola of any kind
Buckwheat
Cakes, biscuits, confectionary
Corn products – popcorn, polenta, corn thins, maize
Couscous
Crackers, cracker breads
Millet
Pastas, noodles
Rice
Rice cakes
Sorghum
Spelt
Thickening agents such as gravy powder, maize starch or stock cubes

BEVERAGES

Beer, cider
Fizzy drinks of any description other than carbonated water
Lite, zero, diet drinks of any description

DAIRY/DAIRY-RELATED

Cheese spreads, commercial spreads
Coffee creamers
Commercial almond milk
Condensed milk
Fat-free anything
Ice cream
Puddings
Reduced-fat cow's milk
Rice milk
Soy milk

FATS

All seed oils (safflower, sunflower, canola, grapeseed, cottonseed, corn)
Chocolate
Commercial sauces, marinades and salad dressings
Hydrogenated or partially hydrogenated oils including margarine, vegetable oils, vegetable fats

FRUITS AND VEGETABLES

Fruit juice of any kind
Vegetable juices (other than home-made with green list vegetables)

GENERAL

All fast food
All processed food
Any food with added sugar such as glucose, dextrose etc

MEAT

All unfermented soya (vegetarian "protein")
Meats cured with excessive sugar
Vienna sausages, luncheon meats

STARCHY VEGETABLES

Beetroots
Legumes
Parsnips
Peanuts
Peas
Potatoes (regular)

SWEETENERS

Agave anything
Artificial sweeteners (aspartame, acusulfame K, saccharin, sucralose, splenda)
Cordials
Dried fruit
Fructose
Honey
Malt
Sugar
Sugared or commercially pickled foods with sugar
Sweets
Syrups of any kind

THE SPEED BUMP

In our experience, some Banters kick off with great weight loss in the first few weeks but soon plateau and struggle to maintain momentum. We find this with Banters who typically have either a lot to lose, are extremely insulin resistant or have been overweight for a very long time. For these Banters, we've developed an extra set of rules to clarify a few grey areas. If you find yourself stuck on a weight-shedding plateau, pay extra special attention to the commandments on the next page.

If you are still not getting the results you would like, consider having blood tests for thyroid imbalance, such as TSH, T4, T3 and antibodies. Find a qualified health professional or knowledgeable integrative GP who knows how to read these imbalances according to the most recent guidelines, and what to do about them. In the case of women having fertility treatment, being on the pill or going through menopause, these all contribute and need to be tweaked for the person concerned – they can potentially play a role in weight loss prevention.

And consider this: stress releases too much cortisol and builds a spare tyre around even a slim waist. So not only can stress lead to you flipping out mentally, but it trips you up physically too.

This is not *The Real Meal Revolution* for nothing. Losing weight is one thing but keeping healthy is something completely different. We want you to eat REAL food. Do your best to stay away from processed junk, regardless of the carb content. It might help you lose weight but who knows what else it does to your body. A rule of thumb: if you can tell what food it is without looking at the package, the chances are that it's real. For example: a chicken nugget does not look like chicken and should be avoided. Chicken breasts look like chicken breasts and should be enjoyed!

WATCH WHAT YOU DRINK

We're faced with a dilemma here. We're trying to promote health and overall well-being so promoting booze is not in our interest as alcohol is highly toxic. Dry wines, most spirits, low energy beers and a few other drinks are safe BUT that is only from a carb perspective. Alcopops, normal beer, any spirit mixer or cocktail will halt any weight loss you're experiencing. It's easy for us to promote low-carb alcoholic beverages but one needs to remember that a low-carb 5% vol. beer is still 5% toxic. Alcohol is also really good at draining motivation, lowering inhibitions, impairing driving ability and, and, and… So we, the authors, leave drinking to you. Consider this our "drinking disclaimer".

You're a grown-up and how much booze you choose to drink is up to you.

THE TEN COMMANDMENTS OF BEGINNER BANTING

1. **Eat enough fat.** This is central to Banting – animal fat does not make you fat … you need to eat it. Small amounts (your body will tell you how much) make you feel full, which stops you from overeating. It also gives you long-lasting energy so in time you won't have that carb craving.

2. **Eat enough vegetables.** This is high fat, not high protein. Don't forget to eat your greens with every meal.

3. **Don't snack.** Initially, while you're in carb-cold-turkey, you will crave everything and will most likely need to snack to keep your sanity. Once you've come off carbs, the only reason you should feel the need to snack is if you are not eating a fatty enough meal or large enough breakfast. Eventually, snacking and Banting become like oil to water.

4. **Don't lie to yourself.** Eating carbs that are perceived to be proteins, like legumes, peanuts and quinoa, can be detrimental. Pay special attention to the Red list on page 49. A Red-listed item is either toxic or will make you fat and should be avoided at all costs.

5. **Don't over- or under-eat.** New Banters get nervous about the idea of not snacking and end up stuffing themselves completely. Fear not, with a high-enough volume of fat in each meal, a reasonable portion of food should carry you to your next meal time. Even though the theory is that if you eat enough fat you should stay fuller for longer, you should still be careful that you're not forcing down food. Get used to the portion size you need to keep you full and try stick to one serving. Eat slowly, drink water and eat only until full; not starving or stuffed, just full. Get used to eating more substantial, less frequent meals. One serving per meal, one meal at a time!

6. **Don't eat too much protein.** We can't stress this enough. This is not high protein eating. You shouldn't need more than 80g of meat with any meal. The main aim is reducing carbs, then increasing fat. Protein stays the same or it could even decrease.

7. **Be alert.** You could be eating secret carbs in supposed healthy products or premade meals. Check the packaging on everything you eat. Anything containing more than 5% carbs should be avoided at all costs. Remember: that diet milkshake you always buy may be low in fat (which is pointless) but it will be loaded with sugar. When you start looking at product labels you'll realise why it's so hard to lose weight. Almost everything has sugar in it! In *The Real Meal Revolution*, we keep it even simpler – if it even has a label, perhaps avoid it anyway.

8. **Avoid too many fruits and nuts.** Remember firstly that fruit is laced with fructose, which is perceived as "good sugar". Sugar is sugar and regardless of its perceived "goodness", it needs to be controlled. Of course refined sugar is a lot more poisonous, so while natural sugars are less likely to kill you, they will do nothing for weight loss. Berries are safe but should be restricted (refer to the Orange list on page 48) and nuts, while low in carbs, should be restricted too – only a handful as a snack if you absolutely have to. Remember that roasted nuts are not good; raw nuts are great.

9. **Control your dairy.** Although dairy is good for you, it does contain carbs and can be a stumbling block for some. In your Banting beginning, perhaps avoid eating too much dairy. Butter is still good!

10. **Be strong!**

THE RECIPES... MODERN ROOTS

Spanning the scope of BANTING history from our ancient beginnings to the BANTING revival, the following recipes have been designed first and foremost by flavour-obsessed chefs who through their adoption of BANTING have also become serious athletes.

"As chefs, we are programmed to frown upon products like pre-packed pastes, marinades, ready-made stocks and sauces. This being said, the recipes in this book have been written to suit the parameters set out by Noakes and our intrepid nutritionist Sally-Ann Creed. If you can't find an ingredient or you don't feel like crushing, mincing or fermenting, add in something else or a pre-made product you feel comfortable using (we frown upon the non-organic, plastic bottle kind). We encourage you to go for the option that is the most real. We want you to eat real food! Mix it up. Try to modify the recipes, make notes and have fun.

Eating like this will involve A MIND SHIFT. Sadly, a toasted cheese and tomato will no longer be a regular snack (unless you use our carb-free bread on page 74). You'll have to start eating burgers with a knife and fork and finally, you'll find breakfast to be a slightly bigger mission than pouring milk over some deathly and delicious chocolate puffed rice. Soon enough your tastes will change and the Whiz-Pop-Choco-Puffs you used to see as a staple will hold zero appeal both in terms of flavour and what they do for your body.

You might also find yourself spending more than usual on food in the beginning but if you stick to your guns and follow some of our guidelines, your appetite will subside and you'll learn a few tricks to saving money. Just take the hit for the first week or two, you'll notice a huge change once you get over your cold turkey stage of coming off your carbohydrate addiction (and it is an addiction). On the cost front, bear in mind that you are playing a long game here. Think of it this way: what you might be spending now on an increased amount of protein and fats while replacing the cheap processed carbohydrates you have relied on for so long, you will make back in the long run in saved medical costs as your body stays lean and trim, steering clear of the threat of lifestyle diseases like obesity and diabetes.

We have tried to build a collection of recipes that are practical, accessible and that will fit in with your everyday life. A lot of the recipes are probably part of your life already and you just didn't realise they were Banting-friendly.

The key to giving up any element of your diet is to use the next best thing to emulate other ingredients. We've put in some practical substitutes like fake mash potato, fake rice and a good fake noodle recipe. There is even a recipe in here for fake lasagne sheets. For interest's sake, everyone has varying levels of insulin resistance so the rules may not need to be as strict for you. However, the recipes are green listed unless otherwise noted. Feel free to adjust the butter, fat and oil amounts according to your palate.

When we say meat, we mean pasture-fed, when we say vegetable, we mean organic, when we say oil, we mean extra-virgin cold-pressed and finally, we never say starch!

And remember: you are not dieting, you are Banting!

Jonno & David

BASICS/58

BREAKFAST/82

MEAT/106

POULTRY/140

FISH AND SEAFOOD/168

SIDES AND SALADS/198

ENTERTAINING/228

Before you start with the exciting stuff, there are some basics here that will make your transition to Banting a seamless process.

The things you will miss the most like mashed potato, rice, breads, rubbish mass-produced mayo and energy drinks are all replaced here with good healthy substitutes.

Our advice here is to get to grips with the basics as soon as possible. Having these stocked in the freezer will make sticking to your game a hundred times easier.

FINDING AND HARVESTING FATS

When you start Banting, the first thing you'll have to get your head around eating is fat. Everyone has a problem eating fat when they change to Banting. The fat is good. You won't die. You need it. You can now shamelessly eat the fat off of a lamb chop and that delicious crispy chicken skin. Some cuts of meat are up to 40% fat. If you cut the fat off, which you have actually paid for, you are literally throwing money away. You are also throwing perfectly good and necessary food away. Another huge incentive to collect animal fat is the fact that coconut and extra-virgin olive oil cost an arm and a leg. Apart from the dressings, you can swap rendered animal fat for oil in almost every recipe.

If there really is too much fat for you to handle, render it and save it. Anything cooked in animal fat is not only rich and decadent but is also seriously delicious. All the fat that comes off a chicken when you roast it can be stored in the fridge or freezer for months. The excess fat from streaky bacon can be collected or used instantly to fry tomatoes or eggs.

How to render fat of any kind:

Place whatever fat you have accumulated from cleaning your meat or poultry in an oven tray and leave it in the oven at 120 to 140°C for up to an hour. You will know the chunks of fat have finished rendering because they will be crispy right the way through. Simply pour the fat out of the tray into a jar and store until needed.

Another tip to help you save money is the way you buy fat. If you ask your butcher to leave the fat on a piece of meat while he's cleaning it for you, you pay the same price per kilo for the fat. Our advice would be to ask for it cleaned as lean as possible, then only after the steak is clean, ask for the offcuts. The beauty of this is that the butcher can't charge you "prime-cut" price for fat and off-cuts.

Of the animals we normally eat, fish generally have the lowest fat content (salmon and trout higher than normal) and lamb has the highest overall fat content. Pork and beef vary because they have thick layers of fat around their bodies but some cuts are a lot leaner than others. Pork fat or lard is by far the most delicious. If you can get smoked lard from your butcher, it will probably be cheaper than butter and is 10 times more delicious to cook with.

Often when one takes on eating a little more fat than usual, one tends to feel a little overwhelmed and over-rich. Although you do eventually get used to it, it is possible to sooth the richness by drinking hot refreshing drinks. Hot water with lemon slices, ginger and mint is a popular favourite as well as any tea infusions. Avoid powdered shakes and the like.

The richness is weird to start with but in the long haul, it is the richness that will help you balance your energy, lose weight and save you from craving those terrible carbs!

CHOCOLATE FAT SHAKE

The fat shake was the first dish that really put this eating style in perspective for us. Initially the perception was that it had changed from fats being bad to them being okay. When a cyclist said he doesn't leave the house without having his fat shake in the morning. it changed everything. People need fat. especially if they're going to be sweating it out all day. This fat shake recipe is inspired by a blog post on TheHubSA.co.za. an incredibly popular South African online cycling forum.

Helpful hint: fat is used as an appetite suppressant and is not something you need to force down. If you're full after a meal and stay feeling full for hours after a meal. you will not need a fat shake. This is for those who simply cannot control their appetites or for those who wish to eat less. Don't force it down. For that matter. don't force anything down. Eat until satisfied.

150ml full-cream milk • 50g butter • 50ml cream • 200ml coconut cream
1 tbsp sugar-free hot chocolate (or a good chunk of 80% couverture or some cocoa powder)
¼ tsp salt

1/ For the hot version. warm all the ingredients in a small saucepan. then blitz with a stick blender.
2/ For the cold one. simply blitz and enjoy.

Note: Using the above base. you can add any flavouring you like. Fresh or frozen berries. vanilla extract or even some almond or macadamia nut butter are all good flavourings. Also. feel free to add a sachet of xylitol or stevia if you want more sweetness.

MAKES 1

BROTHS

The bones of animals contain heaps of minerals, which help prevent cramping and assist with a number of other ailments. **The tip here is to hang on to bones wherever possible.** The moment a chicken carcass is carved or the lamb leg is cleaned, just pop the bones into a pot, cover them with water and leave them on the stove on the lowest temperature for up to 12 hours. Once it is strained, you can boil it for as long as you like to reduce the volume and concentrate the flavours. When you buy fish, ask your fishmonger for the bones and do the same as above. The only difference is that with fish stock, you shouldn't simmer it for more than 40 minutes as it tends to become bitter. Freezing these broths is completely safe. They can be used for soups and sauces of any kind.

In this section, you'll find a basic broth recipe that you can use for any kind of bones, including fish or shellfish (apart from trout, tuna, tilefish and swordfish), lamb, beef or pork. On top of the basic recipe, there are a few slightly more extravagant things to try when you're bored of the bog standard. The best broths on earth are made in Thailand, which is ironic because less than five percent of the population plays sport. Nonetheless, there is a reasonable Thai influence in most of the broths in this book.

BASIC BROTH

Helpful hint: it is 100% normal for a layer of scum and fat to collect on the surface of your stock or broth. The rule of thumb here is if the fat or scum is murky it should be skimmed off the top and thrown out, but if it is clear or golden it should be kept. You can either scoop it off the top and use it for sautéing at a later stage or simply drink it with the broth as it is.

500g bones of any kind · 1 carrot · ½ onion
1 stick celery · 1 bay leaf · 5 peppercorns · 1 head garlic

1/ If the bones are not already roasted, roast them in the oven until they are lightly browned.
You can use them raw, but the roasted flavour is delicious.
2/ Place everything, as is, into a medium-sized pot and cover with water.
Place on the lowest heat and let it tick away for up to 12 hours.
3/ When you taste the broth, it should taste strongly of the animal the bones came from
(you should taste beef if you used beef bones).
4/ Avoid boiling the broth: it makes it go murky, which makes it look unappetising.
But more importantly, it gives it a slightly slimy mouth feel.
5/ Once the broth has taken on the flavour, strain it through a sieve and freeze or use it straight away.

Note: The bone boiling part is the most important. The carrot, onion, celery and other flavourings can be added at a later stage if you don't have them on hand. Also, each protein has certain complementary herbs and spices, which you're encouraged to play with. Fish broth does well with lemon and white wine, beef does well with rosemary, and chicken is good with thyme. Be creative!

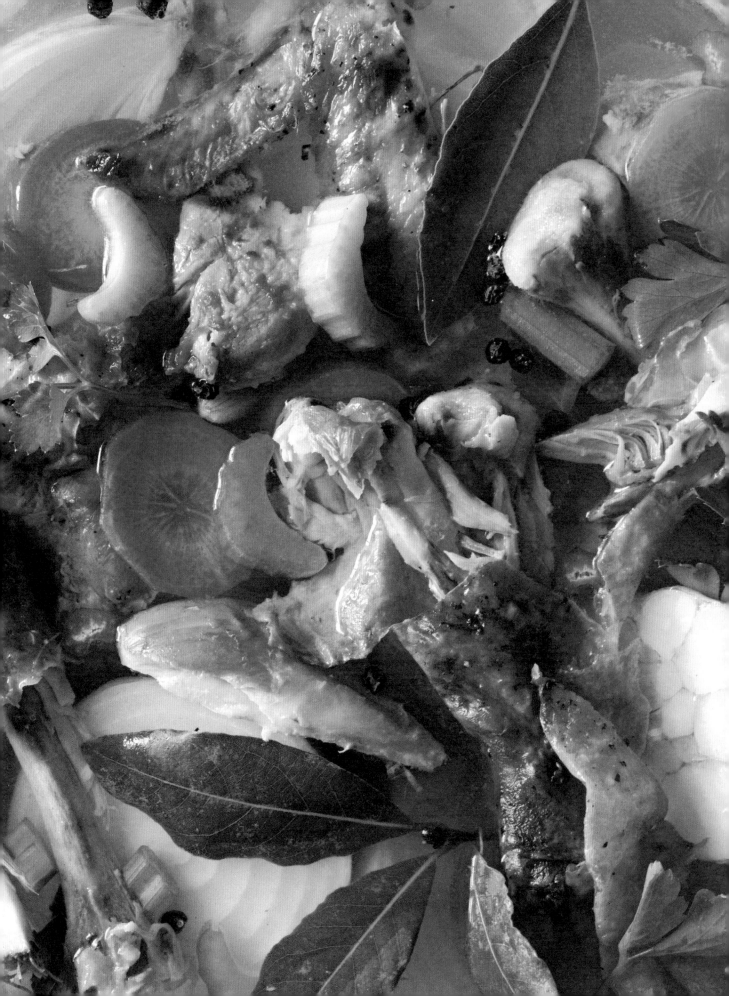

CAULIFLOWER RICE OR "CAULI-RICE"

Just like mashed potato, rice is one of those side dishes that very few people are able to go without. Cauli-rice is a non-grain grain you can now eat as much as you like with no shame!

1kg cauliflower • 1 onion • 100g butter or coconut oil

1/ In a food processor, pulse the cauliflower until you reach couscous consistency.
2/ Melt the butter or coconut oil in a heavy-based frying pan and sauté the onion until soft.
3/ Add the cauliflower and mix through the onion and butter. Leave the heat on low or medium and place the lid on top of the pan.
4/ Leave to cook for five to eight minutes and either set aside or serve immediately.

Note: Just like normal rice, you can add just about anything to cauli-rice. You will need to adjust the water content if you are reading off a rice recipe as the cauli-rice requires no water to cook. It also doesn't hold its texture very well over long cooking periods so things like paella or risotto will need the rice added at the end rather than at the beginning.

SERVES 6

MASHED CAULIFLOWER
OR "CAULI-MASH"

This is one of the fundamentals of Banting and Paleo eating. By cheating the eyes you cheat the mind and it starts with lying to your eyes about mashed potatoes. In restaurants, cauliflower mash is often served as a fancy substitute to standard issue mash, but this is now the standard.

1 head (1kg) cauliflower, broken into florets • 300ml milk
100g butter • salt and pepper

1/ Steam the cauliflower until it is mushy. (Never boil your veggies: this literally washes the nutrients away.)
2/ Using a stick blender or food processor, purée the cauliflower until smooth.
3/ Continue to purée, add the milk, then the butter and beat until smooth and silky.
4/ Season to taste and serve.

Note: Just like mashed potatoes, you can flavour cauliflower with mustard, wasabi, garlic or other flavour profiles.

SERVES 6

CARB-FREE PASTA

Check out http://realmealrevolution.com/free-stuff for a quick video of how
to get this pasta perfect every time.

4 eggs • 125g cream cheese • ½ cup psyllium husks

1/ In a food processor, blend all the ingredients and leave the mixture to thicken for 10 minutes.
2/ Using coconut flour for dusting, roll the pasta into sheets and set aside.
They can be frozen between greaseproof paper or cooked immediately.
3/ Cook as you would normal pasta (be careful, they cook quickly).

COURGETTE NOODLES

Courgette noodles are the best option for Banting or Paleo pasta. They hold their shape nicely and have good flavour. The other great thing about courgettes is that they go well with almost every flavour profile. You really can serve them with anything.

400g large courgettes (the bigger they are. the easier they are to slice)
2 tsp fine salt • 1 tbsp coconut oil

1/ Cut the courgettes into noodles. mix them with the salt and leave them in a colander in the sink for about 20 minutes to drain any excess moisture. You can julienne by either using a knife. a mandoline. a shredder/peeler or a Chinese slicer.
2/ Warm the coconut oil in a large pan and add the courgettes. Sauté them for a few minutes until they are just cooked. then add them to whatever you like.

Note: You could use these noodles as a substitute for any pasta with any pasta sauce. in any Asian broth or a stir-fry or on their own as a light side with some grilled chicken or fish.

SERVES 2

CARB-FREE BREAD

Bread is by far the hardest thing in life to go without once you start Banting. It's also near on impossible to find zero-carb bread that actually has zero carbs, let alone one that tastes good. This recipe ticks all of those boxes as well as being "toastable", which is an added bonus. You may now eat toasties again! Just a note on flaxseed: buy the seeds whole and grind them in a coffee grinder. They go rancid VERY fast!

Helpful hint: this recipe has given a few readers problems when they have combined the ingredients by hand. We recommend using a food processor to make the mixture. This will guarantee the best possible combining of the baking powder and assist in better rising of the bread. Raising agents are also prone to losing their chemical properties when left for too long, so be sure to use only fresh ingredients. We've put together a video to help those people still struggling. Go to: http://realmealrevolution.com/free-stuff for Jonno's fail-safe method.

2 cups milled flaxseed (this recipe will flop if you use pre-ground flax meal.)
5 egg whites • 2 whole eggs • 5 tbsp coconut oil or olive oil
1 tsp baking powder • 1 tsp salt • ½ cup water • 3g stevia

1/ Preheat the oven to 180°C.
2/ In a food processor, blend the dry ingredients together.
3/ Add the wet ingredients to the food processor and blend them together until a batter is formed. Pour the mixture into a greased bread tin and bake until it is cooked through the middle. You can use a skewer to test this, but it usually takes 30 minutes.
4/ Tip it out onto a cooling rack and use as needed. It will slice much better once it has cooled, but it doesn't keep for very long. I recommend slicing it and storing it in the freezer.

Note: This is a completely basic "dough" recipe. You can add any flavouring you like along with other more bulky additives like cheeses or vegetables.
For example, blue cheese and butternut go amazingly well in this bread.
This whole loaf contains 47g of carbs! You could eat the whole loaf and stay a-Banting.

CARB-FREE TORTILLAS
OR "CAULI-WRAPS"

Cauli-wraps are another superb "fake carb" for which we owe thanks to the cauliflower. They won't keep as long as a standard tortilla so you'll want to freeze them and defrost as needed. Check out the "videos" section on http://realmealrevolution.com/free-stuff for a quick video of how to get these tortillas perfect every time.

Tips on how to make perfect tortillas:
- This dough is not a normal dough as it contains ZERO gluten so you need to be VERY gentle when rolling it out. (Gluten is the stuff that holds dough together and makes it stretchy.)
- Smaller. gentler rolling actions are less likely to damage the dough while you roll it out. Lifting the dough. turning it and dusting it regularly will increase your odds of a perfect tortilla.
- You will need a liberal dusting of flour as this is not a normal dough that gets tougher as it is kneaded.
- Coconut flour is better than almond flour and almond flour is hellishly expensive.
- It makes a big difference to add the psyllium to the mix while it is as warm as possible.

500g cauliflower. cut into florets • 4 tbsp psyllium husks • 2 eggs • ¼ tsp salt • coconut flour

1/ Steam or boil the cauliflower until it is completely mushy.
2/ Drain off ALL excess moisture then. using a stick blender or food processor. puree the cauliflower until smooth.
3/ Add the husks. eggs and salt. and blend again. It is VITALLY important to use a blender for this as it guarantees the maximum effect of the psyllium husk. which is the gluten-like binding agent.
4/ Leave it to stand for no less than 15 minutes to thicken into dough.
5/ Break the dough into six balls and roll our each one into a tortilla shape. Use the coconut flour for dusting.
6/ In a heavy based pan. dry fry each tortilla on a medium heat until nicely coloured on the outside and cooked in the middle. You could also bake them in the oven. but the edges do tend to dry out.

Note: For the same. if not better. results. you could substitute butternut or sweet potato for the cauliflower. Just be aware that the carb content shoots up a fair amount.

MAKES 6

BANTING MAYO

Almost all the mayonnaises you get in the stores are made with veg oils. which are against Banting religion. Stay away from all of them and make your own safe and delicious mayo. You can add anything to it just like a normal mayo so go wild with flavour combinations.

1 whole egg • 2 egg yolks • 1 tbsp dijon mustard • juice of 1 lemon
½ cup coconut oil. extra-virgin or refined • ½ cup quality olive oil
1 tbsp double thick greek yoghurt • salt and pepper

1/ Combine the eggs. mustard and lemon juice in a food processor.
2/ Melt the coconut oil in a small pot until it turns to liquid.
Avoid heating it too much or it will cause the eggs to curdle.
3/ Turn the food processor to a fast speed and slowly pour the
coconut oil and olive oil into the egg mixture.
4/ Once the mayo has emulsified. add the yoghurt and season to taste.
This should keep for about a week in the fridge.

Note: If you bulk this up with yoghurt you can make it go a lot further.
Coconut oil is outrageously expensive so it needs to be stretched as far as possible.

MAKES 400ML

FERMENTED PICKLES

FOR THE PICKLING SPICE MIXTURE:
1 stick cinnamon. broken up • 1 tbsp black peppercorns
1 tbsp yellow mustard seeds • 1 tsp fennel seeds
2 tsp whole allspice • 2 tsp coriander seed • 1 tbsp dill seeds

1/ Combine all the ingredients and store in a jar.

Note: In all honesty. you could literally use a teaspoon of mustard seeds. The spices are up to you entirely.

FOR A BASIC PICKLE:
brine • 1l water
70g salt (try use crystal salt: often iodated salt makes the brine go murky)

TO PICKLE
1kg veggies you wish to pickle • 1 tbsp pickling spice mixture of your choice
1 vine leaf • brine to cover

1/ Clean the veg in fresh water and set aside to dry.
2/ In a small saucepan. bring the water. salt and spices to the boil. Leave them to cool.
3/ Pack the veg as tightly as possible into sterilised jars and cover with brine.
Make sure there is a piece of vine leaf in each jar.
4/ Leave them at room temperature (18 to 22°C) for three or four days. Bubbles will begin forming.
This is normal. just skim them off and top with more water or brine if you need to.
5/ You may need to weigh the veg down with another jar in the beginning to keep them submerged.
Once fermentation gets deep into the flesh. they will start sinking. After three weeks. your pickles
should be completely finished. You can keep them in the fridge from this point with the lids on.
From now on. they will stay edible while they slowly continue fermenting.
To keep them fresher for longer. you can drain them and transfer them to new sterilised jars.
Bring the same pickling brine to a boil and pour it back into the jars and close.
When they are finished. the veggies should be opaque. crunchy and tart.
Slimy. mushy veggies are the result of botched fermentation and are spoilt. Sadly. you'll have to chuck them.

Note: The vine leaves are an insurance policy. They help keep the pickles fresh and crunchy.
The fermenting brine is hugely nutritious and is said to be an epic hangover cure.
Some dried or fresh chilli in the pickling mix would also add a nice kick.

fermented pickles were originally invented to increase the shelf life of food. These days, we just pickle because it tastes good. What we often forget is how good real, home-made natural pickles are for our gut flora. **Live bacteria from fermented foods can instantly improve your metabolism and beef up your existing gut flora.** Sterilisation is often a necessary step in the pickling process, which kills the bacteria. Although this does kill all the good guys, the fermentation process changes the nature of the nutrients into a state that will encourage your probiotic cultures to multiply.

Remember that the only thing you can't change is the salt/veg/water ratios in these recipes; they're the scientific parts. You can change all of the flavourings, herbs and spices to your liking. The gherkin is the most popular brined pickle on earth. Before corporates got hold of them and started using vinegar to add fake sourness, all of the acidity came from natural fermentation in a brine solution. On the left, we have given you a spice mixture that you can use to pickle just about anything. The brine recipe we've given you uses a 7% salt content. In colder climates, it is safe to use low salt brine like 4% or 5%. Here in Africa, a slightly higher salt content controls the fermentation. It just keeps everything from going a little too wild in the jar. You can use this brine on absolutely any vegetable you would like to pickle.

Most people find **breakfast** to be the hardest thing to adjust to. When you're tired and want to do the bare minimum to feed yourself in the morning, it is VERY hard to muster up the energy to cook something, especially every day. What you will find is, if you do breakfast properly and get the right amount of fat, you won't really need to eat until mid- to late-afternoon. You will also find your energy levels to be a lot more consistent. This is incredibly different to the peaks and troughs you experience with a cereal kick-start. The good news is that after a few weeks of no carbs, you'll find it much easier to get out of bed, light the stove and push on through. Adding to that, if you start your day with a good, green-listed breakfast, you will stay motivated to stick to it for the rest of the day.

SMOKED MACKEREL WITH AVO AND LEMON/84

KALE WITH CHORIZO AND EGGS/86

EGGS BACONNAISE/88

TROUT AND CREAM CHEESE OMELETTE/90

BACON, ASPARAGUS AND SOFT-BOILED EGGS/92

BLACK MUSHROOMS BAKED IN WALNUT BUTTER
WITH DOUBLE THICK CREAM/94

BACON FAT CHERRY TOMATOES WITH BOCCONCINI/96

"BLITZ RITZ" OR RIPE AVOCADO, CREAM CHEESE AND ANCHOVIES/98

BLUEBERRY AND CREAM CHEESE HOTCAKES/100

COCONUT AND ALMOND FRAPPUCCINO/101

DOUBLE CREAM YOGHURT, ALMOND AND
STRAWBERRY SMOOTHIE/102

AVOCADO AND RASPBERRY SHAKE/102

NUT GRANOLA/104

SMOKED MACKEREL
WITH AVO AND LEMON

This is more of a shopping recipe than a cooking recipe.
If you have the ingredients, there's nothing to it.

6 peppered smoked mackerel fillets • 2 ripe avocados
1 lemon • black pepper • maldon salt • extra-virgin olive oil

1/ Break the mackerel up on a plate.
2/ Slice the avocado and scatter it over the mackerel.
3/ Squeeze over the lemon and give it a good crack of black pepper.
a sprinkle of maldon salt and a decent splash of oil.

If you want to beef it up a little. add a boiled egg. spring onions or rocket.

SERVES 4

KALE WITH CHORIZO AND EGGS

Kale has somehow been forgotten about over the last 20 years.
It has such a lot to offer nutritionally and is about half the price of spinach.
yet hardly anyone knows what to do with it. Because kale is much stronger
in flavour than spinach. it needs to be teamed up with big flavour like
chorizo or other pungently flavoured ingredients.
Having said this. you could still easily swap the spinach for kale.

200g raw kale (or spinach). washed and cut • 1 "horse shoe" chorizo. thickly sliced
⅓ cup water • 80g butter • 8 eggs

1/ Warm the butter in a heavy-based pan with a lid. Gently fry the chorizo
in the butter until it turns golden brown.
2/ Remove the chorizo but keep all the fat and butter in the pan.
3/ Crank the heat up to high and fry the kale in the fat until it begins to wilt.
4/ Pour in the water and allow it to boil ferociously until it is almost fully reduced.
If you use a good heavy-based pan and the heat is right.
this shouldn't take more than a minute.
5/ Shape the kale into a nest in the pan and crack your eggs on top of it.
Cover and cook gently for three minutes.
6/ When you remove the lid. the eggs should be opaque.
Slide the kale off the pan and garnish with the crispy chorizo.
7/ Finally. be sure to pour any excess juices from the pan over each serving.

SERVES 4

EGGS BACONNAISE

A firm favourite with *The Real Meal Revolution*, this is the Banting man's version
of Eggs Benedict but better. Instead of using butter for the hollandaise,
you use the fat from frying the bacon. Whoever thought of using bacon fat to make mayonnaise
should be knighted. As you embark on Banting, you might find yourself shedding a tear
or two for all the bacon fat you've drained onto paper towel over the years. This recipe is perfect
for a special occasion or perhaps a good "healing" meal on a morning after a night before
because it takes slightly longer than a quick flash in the pan and the methods
are slightly more complex. You will need time.

2 small aubergines, grated on the large grain • 300g melted butter
250g streaky bacon • 12 eggs • 1 lemon • 1 tbsp strong dijon mustard
salt and pepper • vinegar

1/ Soak the aubergine in 1 tbsp salt and leave to drain for 30 minutes before
ringing aubergine out and shaping it into large cakes.
2/ In a heavy-based saucepan, fry the aubergine cakes on a low heat with 100g of butter for about
30 minutes, turning carefully now and then.
3/ Place a small pot of water on the stovetop. Give it a splash of vinegar and bring to a boil.
4/ Fry your bacon rashers on a medium heat (so the fat doesn't burn) in the remaining
200g of butter until crispy. Remove from the heat, draining the excess fat back into the pan.
5/ Separate four eggs and place the yolks, lemon juice and mustard in a heat-proof bowl on top of the boiling
vinegar and water (this is called a double boiler). Whisk vigorously until it becomes light and fluffy.
6/ While whisking continuously, slowly pour the melted butter and bacon fat into the egg mixture. Be careful
not to pour it in too fast as the mixture will split. Once you have poured in all of the butter and bacon fat and
it has emulsified, your Baconnaise is ready and can be seasoned and set aside.
7/ Reduce the water temperature to a light simmer. Swirl the water to create a medium-strength circular
current. Break the remaining eggs into a small bowl and tip them, one by one, into the heart of the "whirl pool".
Allow them to poach for about three or four minutes or until soft.
8/ When they're cooked, use a slotted spoon to remove the eggs from the water
and dab them with a dry cloth or paper towel before serving.
9/ By this time, the rostis should be nice and crispy. Remove them from the pan and dab them on paper towel.
10/ Place a rosti on each plate, top each one with bacon, then two eggs and finally, the baconnaise.

Note: A tip for the best poached eggs – use the freshest you can find, they hold their shape the best.
A tip for making baconnaise or hollandaise – if the mixture gets too thick, add a few drops of hot water.
If it starts splitting, do the same and keep whisking. If it splits completely, start again with the lemon,
egg yolk and mustard and use the split sauce as the butter in the first round – pouring it in slowly.

SERVES 4

TROUT AND CREAM CHEESE OMELETTE

Trout and eggs is pretty much a standard on breakfast menus these days. Salmon and trout are interchangeable in this recipe although salmon is slightly higher in omega-3s.

3 eggs • 40g butter • 100g full-fat cream cheese • 80g smoked trout ribbons
lemon wedge • salt and pepper • fresh dill (optional)

1/ Turn the grill on the oven to high.
2/ Place a pan on the stove at medium-high, then add the butter.
3/ Mix the eggs, salt and pepper with a fork. Break the cream cheese into large chunks and add to the egg mixture.
4/ Just as the butter is bubbling and about to change colour, add the egg mixture and stir using a flat-edged lifter. You just want to break up the omelette so the raw egg touches the base of the pan and cooks slightly. Only do this for about 15 seconds.
5/ Place the omelette under the grill until the top layer of egg is just cooked.
6/ Flip the omelette onto a plate and before folding it over, cover the one side with trout, a squeeze of lemon and some dill.
7/ Fold and serve.

Note: The trick to a perfect omelette is getting the pan to the right heat before you add the eggs. A good pan helps too. You could swap trout for bacon and avocado in this one.

SERVES 4

BACON, ASPARAGUS AND SOFT-BOILED EGGS

250g streaky bacon • 200g asparagus spears
8 eggs • 40g butter • salt and black pepper

1/ Place a small pot of water on to boil.
2/ In a heavy-based frying pan, fry the bacon in the butter until crispy,
then remove from the heat.
3/ Drop the eggs into the water (4.5 minutes for perfect soft-boiled eggs)
4/ Blanch the asparagus in the egg water and drop it straight into the bacon pan with the fat,
butter and all that other goodness. If the bacon is off the heat already, that's fine.
5/ As the eggs come out of the water, turn the bacon and asparagus pan back
on and allow the asparagus to colour a little.
6/ Peel the eggs under water. (It is 1 000 times easier this way.)
7/ Serve the bacon, asparagus and the pan juices with the boiled eggs broken over the top.

SERVES 4

BLACK MUSHROOMS BAKED IN WALNUT BUTTER WITH DOUBLE THICK CREAM

Another great vegetarian option here! You could also use this as a side but the meatiness of those big black mushrooms is plenty for brekkie. Also, when you're adding that glorious double thick cream at the end, you'll agree that this dish needs NOTHING else.

4 large or 8 medium black mushrooms • 1 cup walnuts, gently crushed
4 or 8 cloves garlic, left whole (depending on number of mushrooms)
120g butter or lard • 120g double thick cream • salt and pepper

1/ Preheat the oven to 200°C.
2/ Lay the mushrooms out on a baking tray and place one clove
of garlic in the centre of each one.
3/ Mix the nuts and butter together and share equally over each mushroom, on top of the garlic.
4/ Place the mushrooms in the oven for about 15 minutes (or until cooked).
5/ Serve immediately with a big dollop of the thickest, creamiest double thick cream
you can find on each mushroom.

Note: If you're not a fan of whole cloves of garlic, they're whole so you can take them out.
The flavour will have penetrated right through the mushroom anyway.

SERVES 4

BACON FAT CHERRY TOMATOES
WITH BOCCONCINI

This is one of those things you'd throw together when you've got leftover cheese from a little salad the night before. Funnily enough, if not at breakfast, this dish would go down a treat at a pizza party where there aren't any carb-free bases.

250g streaky bacon, cut into four-centimetre strips • 20g bacon fat or butter
1 cup large cherry tomatoes • 250g balls fresh bocconcini (you can break up a piece of buffalo mozzarella into big chunks) • 1 handful fresh basil leaves

1/ Add the bacon and fat to a cold pan, then place on the heat.
2/ Keep the heat on medium-low for about five minutes to let the fat
and juice come out of the bacon.
3/ Once the bacon is crispy, crank the heat up to full, add the tomatoes and stir continuously.
4/ Once the tomatoes and bacon are looking brown on the edges, chuck the cheese balls and basil in, toss for about 10 seconds and serve immediately.

Note: Eat this the moment that cheese goes in. If you leave it for any longer the cheese will melt and you won't get that amazing sensation of a ball of cheese actually melting in your mouth. If you're fresh out of bocconcini, any cheese will do. Brie and Camembert are superb with tomatoes and melt brilliantly.

SERVES 4

"BLITZ RITZ" OR RIPE AVOCADO, CREAM CHEESE AND ANCHOVIES

This is a serious on-the-run breakfast. Probably the best thing about it is how such a small meal can be packed with so much flavour and fill you up so quickly. Season dependent, you can get away with spending very little on this breakfast.

1 large ripe avocado • 2 heaped tbsp full-fat cream cheese • juice of ½ a lemon
red or green tabasco sauce • 10 small, epic-quality anchovy fillets
cracked black pepper

1/ Halve the avo, remove the pip and place each half on a plate.
Top each one with half the cream cheese.
2/ Lay the anchovies on the cream cheese and the flesh of the avo.
Season well with lemon juice, tabasco sauce and black pepper.

Note: No need for salt here, the anchovies should be salty enough. The success of this dish depends entirely on the quality of the anchovies. Poor quality anchovies or pilchards prepared like anchovies can be horrendous and taste like rotten seafood.

SERVES 2

BLUEBERRY AND CREAM CHEESE HOTCAKES

Cooked blueberries are something quite special. When they cook they release a sublime
sweetness and their flavour changes completely. This particular hotcake,
once garnished with the cream cheese, tastes a bit like blueberry cheesecake.
It will make absolutely no difference if you use frozen blueberries.
Check out http://realmealrevolution.com/free-stuff for a quick video
of how to get these hotcakes perfect every time.

½ cup almond flour • ½ cup coconut flour • 1 ⅓ cups ricotta • ¾ cup milk
1 tsp baking powder • 4 eggs, separated • pinch of salt • 180g fresh or frozen blueberries
50g butter • 200g full-fat cream cheese

1/ Combine flours, ricotta, milk, baking powder, egg yolks and salt in a bowl and blitz
with a blender or food processor, then mix the blueberries through the mixture.
2/ Whisk the egg whites to stiff peaks and fold them into the mixture in two batches.
3/ Warm a pan to a medium heat and melt the butter. Fry the hotcakes in
batches of three, using roughly two tablespoons of batter per hotcake.
4/ Top each hotcake with cream cheese as it comes off the heat.

Note: If you're not entertaining, don't bother eating them off a plate, just eat them straight
out of the pan. The hotter they are, the softer the cream cheese gets.

SERVES 4

COCONUT AND ALMOND FRAPPUCCINO

For those who aren't too keen on incredibly rich breakfast shakes and "hash-ups",
this recipe is more like an enriched coffee on the run. It's about as light as a high-fat
meal can get, but it's better than nothing and it should help crush your hunger,
at least until tea time.

1 shot espresso • ½ cup coconut cream • ½ cup full-cream milk
2 tbsp almond butter • ½ cup ice blocks

1/ Pour all the ingredients into a smoothie machine or food processor and blitz until smooth.

Note: You could easily swap the espresso for a teaspoon or two of instant coffee.

SERVES 1

DOUBLE CREAM YOGHURT, ALMOND AND STRAWBERRY SMOOTHIE

This is by far the quickest breakfast recipe in this book, and it's delicious.

1 tbsp almond butter • 150ml double cream yoghurt
100g frozen strawberries • 10 blocks of ice

1/ Place all the ingredients in a food processor or a smoothie machine and blitz.
You could also use a stick blender.

Note: You should be able to get almond butter in the health aisle at most supermarkets.
Alternatively try a health shop, but it's out there. You could also swap the almond butter
for macadamia nut butter if almonds aren't your thing.

SERVES 1

AVOCADO AND RASPBERRY SHAKE

Avocado in a shake, seriously? Believe it. The fresh acidity of the raspberries in this shake
almost completely masks the avocado flavour, leaving behind only the creamy texture.
If you're doing 'Blitz Ritz' for one, this is a good use for the other side of your avocado.

½ ripe avocado, pipped and peeled • 100g frozen raspberries
100g extra-thick Greek yoghurt • squeeze of lemon juice
½ cup ice blocks

1/ Combine all the ingredients in a food processor or smoothie machine and blitz.

Note: In all shakes where one would usually use banana, we recommend adding avocado instead.
Bananas pale in comparison to avocados on a nutritional scale, and the texture
of avocados is actually smoother.

SERVES 1

NUT GRANOLA

This "granola" takes the place of any muesli one might want to have with yoghurt.

100g walnuts • 100g sunflower seeds • 100g chopped hazelnuts
100g almond flakes • 3 tbsp coconut oil • 2 tsp cinnamon
2 tsp ginger • ½ tsp nutmeg

1/ Preheat the oven to 160°C.
2/ Chop the nuts roughly and mix them together.
3/ In a large pan, fry the spices in the coconut oil, then add the nuts and toast them briefly.
4/ Tip the nuts onto an oven tray and bake for 10 minutes.
5/ Cool on paper towel and store in an airtight container.

SERVES 12-15

This chapter is, I suppose, what everyone thinks the Banting lifestyle is all about: lots and lots of meat! We've mentioned this in previous chapters, but protein is only a small part of it. You need the nutrients you get from meat but please, by all means, don't use this chapter as your only lunch and dinner guide – it may have an adverse effect on your health. Rather, spend time pairing these recipes with your favourite side dishes from the later chapters.

LIME AND SUMAC RUMP SKEWERS /108

BEEF AND LIME BROTH/110

SMOKY PORK BROTH/112

GRILLED HARISSA LAMB CHOPS WITH TOMATO AND CUCUMBER SALSA /114

BELLY RIBS WITH ORIGANUM AND SMOKED PAPRIKA /116

BEEF STEAK WITH HORSERADISH CRÈME FRAÎCHE AND ROASTED TOMATO SALSA /118

QUICK "TRINCHADO" ON SAUTÉED VEG /120

FIERY BEEF SALAD WITH CASHEWS /122

BEEF AND "CAULI-MASH" SHEPHERD'S PIE /124

PORK LARB SALAD /126

BRAISED BEEF SHOULDER /128

SLOW-ROASTED PORK BELLY WITH ASIAN BASTING /130

DEBONED BUTTERFLIED LEG OF LAMB /132

LAMB AND MUSHROOM BLANQUETTE /134

PORK FILLET STIR-FRY WITH GREEN CHILLI PASTE AND COCONUT MILK /136

BEEF LASAGNE /138

LIME AND SUMAC RUMP SKEWERS

This is another great dish for the braai. Rump doesn't dry out on the fire as fast as other cuts like sirloin. It is also much higher in fat, which is what makes it so juicy.

8 bamboo skewers, soaked in water for at least 15 minutes
480g beef rump, cut into 20g cubes • 6 cloves garlic, crushed • 1 tbsp sumac
3 tbsp extra-virgin olive oil • 1 tsp salt • 1 tsp sesame seeds
1 tsp cinnamon • 1 tsp ground coriander • 1 tsp ground cardamom
1 red onion, cut into large squares • Large mint leaves • 2 limes

1/ Place all the ingredients apart from the onion, mint and limes in a bowl and mix well.
If you have time, leave the mixture to sit for an hour.
2/ Skewer the kebabs with three pieces of rump per skewer, with a sprig of mint
and a slice of red onion between each piece of rump.
3/ Grill on the highest heat possible until medium-rare. Squeeze over some lime
and serve immediately.

Note: This is best served with some really thick yoghurt seasoned with lime juice,
fresh coriander and chilli.

SERVES 4

BEEF AND LIME BROTH

1.2l rich beef broth • 1 large onion, sliced • 2 cloves garlic, minced
2 large tomatoes, cut into six wedges each
2 large red chillies, roughly chopped • 160g green beans, topped and tailed
2 tbsp sweet paprika • 100g baby spinach • 1 handful basil
juice of 2 limes • 1 small handful mint

1/ Sauté the onion in a splash of oil or butter. Add the garlic and stir until fragrant.
Add the stock and bring to a boil.
2/ Add the tomatoes, chillies, green beans and paprika and boil
until the flavours have combined nicely.
3/ Add the spinach, basil, lime juice and mint. Season with salt and pepper.

Note: Some seared steak pieces would "beef" this up if you wanted to have it as a meal.

SERVES 4

SMOKY PORK BROTH

If you haven't thrown your smoky pork hock into your mother's special pea and ham soup. it's recommended you use it for a rich pork broth. Broths are so rarely made using pork bones but the pig has some of the best flavour you can get. You can use smoked or unsmoked bones for your broth. it depends entirely on your palate.

500ml smoky pork stock (or other stock) • 100g gammon steak. sliced
½ red onion. sliced • 1 red pepper. sliced • 1 clove garlic. crushed
80g sugar snaps. halved at an angle • ½ cup cherry tomatoes
½ tsp smoked paprika • juice of 1 lemon • 2 large sprigs origanum. washed and picked

1/ In a saucepan. sauté the gammon. onion and pepper on a medium heat
until the gammon begins to caramelise.
2/ Add the garlic and sauté until aromatic. Add the broth and bring to a boil for five minutes.
3/ Add the sugar snaps. cherry tomatoes. smoked paprika
and lemon juice and simmer for five minutes.
4/ Add the origanum and season to taste with salt and pepper.

Note: This soup does well with anything smoky or porky added in. If you have bacon.
pork belly. some more sausages or even black pudding. chuck it in.

SERVES 2

GRILLED HARISSA LAMB CHOPS
WITH TOMATO AND CUCUMBER SALSA

FOR THE HARISSA PASTE:
8 dried red chillies • 8 cloves garlic, minced • 1 tsp salt • 8 tbsp olive oil
2 tbsp ground coriander • 2 tbsp ground caraway seeds • 1 tbsp cumin seeds

1/ In a pestle and mortar, grind the chillies, garlic, salt and olive oil. Add the remaining spices
and rub to form a smooth paste. Drizzle a little bit of olive oil on top to keep it fresh.
The paste should keep for a month in the fridge if stored in an airtight container.

FOR THE LAMB CHOPS:
8 lamb chops, about two centimetres thick • 1 batch harissa paste

1/ Rub the harissa paste on both sides of the lamb chops, then marinate
in the fridge for at least an hour.
2/ Remove from the fridge and allow the chops to come to room temperature.
It will take about 20 minutes.
3/ Heat a grill pan over high heat until almost smoking. Add the chops and sear
for about two minutes. Flip the chops and cook for another three minutes
for medium-rare and 3.5 minutes for medium.

FOR THE TOMATO AND CUCUMBER SALAD:
3 large firm tomatoes, finely chopped • ½ cucumber, finely diced
1 small red onion, finely chopped • 2 tbsp lemon or lime juice • 2 tbsp olive oil
1 tbsp chopped fresh mint • 1 clove garlic, minced • salt and pepper

1/ Toss all the ingredients together and leave to stand to allow the flavours to infuse.

SERVES 4

BELLY RIBS WITH ORIGANUM
AND SMOKED PAPRIKA

Research has found that sugar-free pork rib recipes are almost
non-existent. But pork ribs (smoked ribs especially) are one of the most delicious
things out there. You need a sugar-free rib if you ever want a braai to be the same again!

2kg belly ribs • 2 cups saved cooking juices (broth or stock)
3 cloves fresh garlic, finely diced • 100g can tomato paste • ¼ cup apple cider vinegar
¼ cup prepared mustard • 1 tsp ground cumin • 2 tsp sea salt • 2 tsp smoked paprika
2 tsp dried origanum • black pepper to taste

1/ Preheat the oven to 180°C.
2/ Combine all the ingredients in a deep tray, being sure to lay the ribs out flat. If the ribs aren't
fully submerged, fill the tray with some water. Cover the tray with foil and cook for two hours.
3/ Remove the tray from the heat and leave the ribs to cool in the juices.
4/ Once cool, drain the liquid into a pot and reduce to a sticky glaze.
5/ Grill the ribs in the oven or on the braai and constantly baste both sides with the glaze.
6/ When the ribs start to go black on the edges, remove them from the heat, cut and enjoy.

Note: This can also be done with loin/back ribs. You could also reduce these ingredients down
without the ribs and use the glaze to baste anything on the braai.

SERVES 4

BEEF STEAK WITH HORSERADISH CRÈME FRAÎCHE AND ROASTED TOMATO SALSA

FOR THE HORSERADISH CRÈME FRAÎCHE:
⅓ cup horseradish, drained or ready-made
⅓ cup crème fraîche or sour cream

1/ Mix the crème fraîche and horseradish in a bowl and leave in the fridge until needed.

FOR THE ROASTED TOMATO SALSA:
5 roma tomatoes • ⅓ cup chopped basil • 2 cloves garlic, minced
1 tbsp fresh lime juice • 1 tbsp balsamic vinegar
2 tsp salt • ½ tsp cracked black pepper • 4 tbsp olive oil

1/ Under a hot grill, roast the tomatoes until the skin is blackened.
Remove charred bits, dice and place in a bowl. Cover and leave to cool for 15 minutes.
2/ Add the basil, garlic and lime juice and marinate for 10 minutes.
3/ Add the vinegar, salt and pepper. Slowly whisk in the olive oil.

FOR THE STEAK:
2 x 300g nice thick-cut steak (rump or sirloin) • salt and freshly ground black pepper
1 tsp coriander, toasted and crushed • olive oil, for searing

1/ Preheat the oven to 220°C.
2/ Season the beef with salt, pepper and coriander and brush with olive oil.
3/ Get a griddle pan smoking hot and sear the steaks until they are brown all over.
Transfer the steaks to a tray and cook them in the oven until medium-rare.
4/ Set aside to rest for 10 minutes.
5/ Re-sear the steak in the pan. Plate with a tablespoon of horseradish mix
on top and serve salsa on the side.

Note: We have garnished with freshly diced tomato in this photo.
The roasted salsa would obviously be a lot saucier!

SERVES 2

QUICK "TRINCHADO" IN SAUTÉED VEG

Trinchado was a favourite snack in Proudfoot's restaurant days. "Any beef offcuts we couldn't serve would go into the daily trinchado lunch, which became a small competition amongst the chefs. If only I had this recipe back then. I might have won it once or twice."

400g rump, cut into 25g cubes • 50g butter • 1 large red onion, roughly chopped
1 tbsp garlic and chilli paste • 1 cup green olives, pitted • 1 cup beef stock
juice of 1 lemon • 1 tsp smoked paprika (preferably hot)
1 large handful Italian parsley, roughly chopped

1/ Get a large heavy-based pan smoking hot.
2/ Oil and season the beef cubes well. Place them in the pan, turn and leave them to colour.
You may need to do this in two batches to prevent the juices coming out of the meat.
3/ Before the meat gets to medium-rare (two minutes), tip the meat into a tray and cool.
4/ Using the same hot pan without cleaning it, add the onion and butter
and sauté until golden brown.
5/ Now add the garlic and chilli paste and sauté it until it becomes aromatic.
6/ Add the olives, beef stock, lemon juice and smoked paprika and boil until reduced by half.
7/ Just before serving, add the parsley and tip the meat back into the pan to warm
through to medium rare/medium.
8/ Serve immediately.

FOR THE SAUTÉED VEG:
1 large red onion, roughly chopped
2 red peppers, roughly chopped • 1 yellow pepper, roughly chopped
4 small courgettes, cut into large pieces • 50g butter • 3 tbsp capers

1/ Sauté the onion, peppers and courgettes in the butter over medium heat
until they begin to caramelise.
2/ Add the capers and serve with trinchado.

SERVES 4

FIERY BEEF SALAD WITH CASHEWS

FOR THE DRESSING:
⅓ cup fresh lime juice • ¼ cup fresh cilantro, chopped • 1 tbsp water
1 tbsp Thai fish sauce • 4 cloves garlic, minced • 1 tsp strong chilli paste
1 large knob ginger, grated

1/ Combine all the ingredients and leave in the fridge to infuse for as long as possible.

FOR THE SALAD:
500g fillet steak • ¼ tsp salt • ⅓ tsp black pepper • extra-virgin olive oil
6 cups cos lettuce, ripped • 1 cup cherry tomatoes, quartered
1 cup spring onion, thinly sliced • ¼ cup fresh mint, coarsely chopped
200g roasted cashew nuts

1/ Place a grill or frying pan on a high heat.
2/ Cut the steak into three and sprinkle both sides with salt and pepper.
3/ Place the steak in the pan, coated with a spoon of olive oil,
and cook for five minutes on each side or until desired degree is reached.
4/ Leave to stand for five minutes, then cut the steak diagonally across the grain
into five-millimetre strips.
5/ Combine steak, lettuce and remaining ingredients in a large bowl.
Add the dressing, toss to coat and serve.

SERVES 4

BEEF AND "CAULI-MASH" SHEPHERD'S PIE

Similar to lasagne, cottage pie is a staple on the home-cooked meal roster.
With potatoes now out of the picture you can make a quick adjustment
and use cauliflower to make that delicious crusty topping.

FOR THE MINCE:

400g beef mince • 125g streaky bacon • 40g butter • 1 large onion, finely chopped
4 celery sticks, roughly chopped • 2-3 cloves garlic, minced • 50g tomato paste
1 cup beef stock • 3 large sprigs thyme, chopped • 200g button mushrooms, sliced
1 tin chopped tomatoes • 3 large sprigs origanum, chopped • salt and pepper

1/ In a medium-sized, heavy-based frying pan, sauté the mince and bacon in the butter until golden brown.
2/ Once the mince has browned, remove the meat, leaving the fat in the pan, and add the onion and celery.
3/ Sauté the onion and celery in the fat until golden brown. Add the garlic and sauté until aromatic.
4/ Return the mince to the pan, add the tomato paste and stir until a dark sediment collects
on the base of the pot (this sediment gives the mince an amazing roasted flavour).
5/ Add the beef stock, thyme, mushrooms and tinned tomato and simmer on a low heat
for about an hour to cook and reduce.
6/ Add the origanum and season to taste with salt and pepper.

FOR THE CAULI-MASH:

1 cauliflower head, broken into florets • 100g butter • 2 egg yolks • ground nutmeg

1/ Steam the cauliflower until it goes mushy.
2/ Place the cauliflower in a food processor and purée until smooth.
3/ While the blender is running, add the egg yolks.
4/ Add in the butter, one knob at a time until it has melted and the mixture is smooth.
5/ Season with nutmeg to taste.

TO MAKE THE COTTAGE PIE:

1/ Fill a lasagne/pie dish with the mince and smooth it out.
2/ Top it with the cauliflower purée and press the classic fork pattern into the top.
3/ Place it under the grill for 15 minutes until golden brown.

Note: You can add anything exciting into the mince that you think will add to the flavour!
If you need a little extra fat, you can always give the crust a generous sprinkling of cheese.

SERVES 4

PORK LARB SALAD

This is a traditional Thai dish. It's seriously easy to make and will soon become
a favourite lunch option.

400g fatty pork mince (at least 20% fat) • 3 tbsp chilli. garlic and ginger paste (or 1 tbsp of
each. chopped) • ½ stick lemongrass. grated or finely chopped • 1 tsp Chinese five spice powder
¼ tsp cardamom • 1 small bunch spring onion • juice of 1 lime • 1 tbsp fish sauce
½ handful fresh coriander. roughly chopped • ½ handful fresh basil. roughly chopped
4 large cos lettuce leaves

1/ In a large. heavy-based pan. fry the mince until golden brown.
The mince should release its own fat so there is no need to add extra fat.
2/ Add the chilli paste. lemongrass. Chinese five spice and cardamom and fry until dark brown.
3/ Add the spring onion. fish sauce. lime juice. coriander and basil and stir for a minute.
4/ Serve the mince as you would a taco. using the lettuce leaf as the taco shell.

SERVES 2

BRAISED BEEF SHOULDER

1.6kg beef shoulder or fore rib • 1 cup carrots, roughly chopped
1 cup onion, roughly chopped • ½ cup celery, roughly chopped • 4 cups warm chicken stock
3 cups red wine • 1 garlic bulb, cloves removed and peeled • ½ cup fresh thyme
1 tbsp salt • 1 cup fresh double cream • ¼ cup horseradish

1/ Season the beef shoulder all over with salt and pepper, then brown in a large
heavy pot over a medium heat.
2/ Once browned on all sides, add vegetables and enough stock and wine
to cover the roast, along with the garlic and thyme.
3/ Cook at 160°C until the meat is tender and comes apart with no resistance
(about three hours). Make sure the pot itself is tightly wrapped in tin foil.
4/ When the meat is tender, remove the roast to a platter to cool for 10 minutes.
Reserve the beef broth.
5/ Wrap the beef tightly in aluminium foil, forming an oblong shape. Place in the fridge to set.
6/ To prepare the sauce, boil the broth for 20 minutes and strain into another pot.
7/ Mix in the cream thoroughly and reduce to thicken.
8/ When the desired thickness is reached, season to taste with salt and pepper.
(It can be stored in the fridge.)
9/ Remove the cold braised shoulder from the fridge, unwrap and
cut into two-centimetre-thick slices.
10/ Fry off the slices in butter until golden brown.
11/ Warm the sauce and add the horseradish.
12/ Serve the meat with a good coating of creamy sauce.

Note: You can add a number of different flavourings to the sauce such as Dijon
or hot mustard, rosemary or roast garlic.

SERVES 8

SLOW-ROASTED PORK BELLY
WITH ASIAN BASTING

This is another slow-cooked option. Perhaps not the best idea for an early dinner but if you're heading out for a mid-Sunday-morning run, this will be perfect by the time you get back (depending on how fit you are of course).

FOR THE ROAST VEGETABLE BASE:
2 onions, roughly chopped • ½ bunch celery, chopped • 5 carrots, chopped
2 sweet potatoes, cubed, skin on

1/ Place the vegetables on the base of a tray, clustered together to fit the shape of the slab of pork belly.

FOR THE ASIAN GLAZE:
3 tbsp soy sauce • 1 tbsp red wine vinegar • 1 tbsp hoisan sauce

1/ Mix the ingredients together in a bowl.

FOR THE PORK:
1.6kg pork belly • 1 tsp salt • 1 tbsp honey • 2 cloves garlic, chopped
1 tsp dried origanum • 1 tsp ground cumin • 1 tsp ground coriander
1 tsp dried thyme • 1 tbsp olive oil

1/ Preheat the oven to 220°C.
2/ In a mortar and pestle or food processor, grind the salt, honey, garlic, herbs and olive oil into a paste.
3/ Rub the belly with the spices and place on the nest of veggies.
4/ Pour two cups of water into the tray and place in the oven for 20 minutes.
5/ Turn the temperature down to 160°C and cook for one hour and 40 minutes, basting the belly every 20 minutes with the pan juices and Asian glaze.
6/ Serve immediately, using the pan juices as gravy and the veg nest as a side.

SERVES 8

DEBONED BUTTERFLIED LEG OF LAMB

This recipe calls for two sets of flavourings. First you marinate the leg
in the fridge to penetrate the meat. then it gets a thick spice rub that
adds a beautiful crust while the lamb cooks on the fire or in the oven.

FOR THE MARINADE:
1.2kg boneless leg of lamb. butterflied • ¼ cup olive oil • 3 tbsp fresh lemon juice
4 cloves garlic. minced • 2 tbsp fresh origanum. chopped • 1 tbsp fresh rosemary. chopped
½ tsp salt • ½ tsp ground black pepper

1/ In a bowl. whisk together the oil. lemon juice. garlic. origanum. rosemary. salt and pepper.
2/ Pour over the lamb and rub evenly across the surface. Leave in the fridge. covered. for
at least two hours (it can be left for up to six hours – turn occasionally).

FOR THE PASTE:
2 cloves garlic • ½ onion. finely chopped • 1 tbsp paprika
1 tbsp coarse salt • ½ tbsp black pepper • ½ tbsp cayenne pepper
1 tbsp dry origanum • 1 tbsp dried thyme • 2 tbsp olive oil

1/ Combine all ingredients and pound to a smooth paste in a pestle and mortar or food processor.

FOR THE LAMB:
1/ Light a fire or preheat the oven to 180˚C.
2/ Remove the lamb from the fridge and let it come to room temperature.
3/ Season generously on all sides with the paste.
4/ Braai the leg for about 40 minutes on relatively cool coals. turning regularly
(or roast in the oven). The meat should be medium to medium-rare.
5/ Remove from the braai and transfer to a platter. Cover with foil and allow
to rest for 10 minutes before carving.

Note: For the oven. simply roast it for about 40 minutes.
You could serve this with any side but we recommend some chargrilled aubergines.

SERVES 6

LAMB AND MUSHROOM BLANQUETTE

This is one of the few stews where you don't brown the meat first.
You actually don't brown anything off. which is why this is by far the
quickest stew one can make. It also happens to be seriously good.

600g lamb shoulder. cut into cubes • 2 onions. halved • 4 celery sticks. cut into chunks
5 sprigs thyme • 5 sprigs rosemary • 2 garlic heads. halved
2 cups chicken stock • 1 cup white wine • 50ml cream
250g white or button mushrooms. whole
200g butter

1/ Preheat the oven to 180˚C.
2/ Place the lamb. onions. celery. thyme. rosemary. garlic. stock and wine in an
ovenproof casserole dish. Cover with foil and place it in the oven for two and half hours.
3/ Check the meat to see whether it is soft and tender. If it is still tough. pop it back
in the oven for another 30 minutes.
4/ Once it is melt-in-the-mouth tender. use a sieve to drain the liquid into a pot.
then reduce. Include all of the juices from the tray. fat included.
5/ Once the liquid has reduced to 400ml. add the cream and mushrooms and
reduce until thick and creamy (about 400 to 500ml).
6/ Once the sauce is thick and the mushrooms are tender. add back the meat.
add the butter and stir until it has melted and emulsified.
7/ Season with salt and pepper and serve.

Note: This stew goes brilliantly with buttered broccoli. or broccoli of any kind for that matter.

SERVES 4

PORK FILLET STIR-FRY WITH GREEN CHILLI PASTE AND COCONUT MILK

400g pork fillet. thinly sliced • 3 tsp Thai green curry paste
3 cloves garlic. finely chopped • ¼ cup coriander. chopped • 1 tbsp coconut oil
2 tbsp oyster sauce • 1 tbsp fish sauce • ½ cup chicken stock
200ml coconut milk • ½ cup carrot. shredded • ½ cup spring onion. shredded
½ cup mange tout. shredded • ⅓ cup basil leaves. thinly sliced

1/ Combine the green curry paste. garlic and coriander in a small bowl and mix well.
2/ Heat the oil in a wok. swirling to coat the surface. Add the curry mixture and stir-fry
until garlic is aromatic. about one minute.
3/ Add the pork and stir-fry. stirring often. until meat is cooked (about five minutes).
4/ Add the oyster sauce. fish sauce. chicken stock and coconut milk.
Stir to combine and heat thoroughly.
5/ Add the shredded vegetables and toss for one minute.
6/ Stir in the basil leaves and serve immediately.

SERVES 4

BEEF LASAGNE

Lasagne is an absolute classic home-cooked meal: a simple pleasure that is sorely missed when one gives up carbs. You could use the carb-free pasta recipe on page 70 but when you make lasagne at home, you probably use bought pasta, so expecting you to start making your own might be a big ask. The advice there would be to use sliced aubergine or courgettes as your pasta sheets. Be sure to put them in raw so they suck in all the juices from the meat and white sauce.

FOR THE MINCE:
250g streaky bacon • 400g fatty beef mince • 40g butter
2 large onions, finely chopped • 2-3 cloves garlic, minced • 50g tomato paste
½ cup red wine • 1 cup beef stock • 3 large sprigs thyme, chopped
1 tin chopped tomatoes • 1 tbsp Worcestershire sauce
3 large sprigs origanum, chopped • salt and pepper

1/ In a medium-sized, heavy-based frying pan, sauté the bacon and mince in the butter until golden brown.
2/ Once the mince is brown, remove the meat, leaving the fat in the pan, and add the onions.
Sauté the onions in the fat until golden brown.
3/ Add the garlic and sauté until aromatic.
4/ Add back the mince along with the tomato paste and stir until a dark sediment collects
on the base of the pot (this sediment gives the lasagne an amazing roasted flavour).
5/ Once a good sediment has collected, add the red wine and reduce by half.
6/ Add the beef stock, thyme and tinned tomatoes and simmer on a low heat for about an hour.
7/ Add the Worcestershire sauce and origanum and season to taste with salt and pepper.

FOR THE CHEESE SAUCE:
2 cups cream • 4 cups grated cheese (cheddar or a harder cheese like Parmesan)
salt and pepper • pinch grated nutmeg • grated cheese for the top

1/ Bring the cream to the boil, then add in the cheese, reduce the heat and
stir continuously until the cheese has melted and sauce is a good cheesy consistency.
2/ Season with salt, pepper and nutmeg.

TO MAKE THE LASAGNE:
1/ Lay sheets of "pasta" on the base of a lasagne dish (see page 70 for the carb-free pasta recipe).
Cover the sheets with a third of the mince, then cover with a layer of pasta.
2/ Add another layer of mince, then pasta.
3/ Add the final layer of mince and top with the cheese sauce and a layer of grated cheese on top.
4/ Bake in the oven at 180°C for 30 minutes.

SERVES 6

In South Africa, our variety of **poultry** is quite limited. Turkeys only really come around once a year and ducks are hellishly expensive. One of the reasons is that chickens are manufactured at such an alarming rate that hardly anything can compete price-wise. As you will have read earlier in this book, we are completely anti this kind of farming. When you use chicken, duck or turkey in any of the recipes that follow, choose the organic ones. All "free-range" means is that they're not in cages, but they still walk around in massive pens and are given heaps of growth hormones. On a lighter note, organic chickens are still cheaper than most other meats.

CHERMOULA CHICKEN KEBABS WITH DUKKHA YOGHURT/142
NOT BUTTER CHICKEN /144
CHICKEN TIKKA MASALA/146
PARMESAN CHICKEN PIECES WITH ROAST
GARLIC TOMATO MOLE/148
CHICKEN LIVERS PERI-PERI/150
ROAST CHICKEN/152
GRILLED CHICKEN SALAD WITH SUNDRIED TOMATOES
AND "RANCH DRESSING"/154
ROAST DUCK/156
KUNG PAO CHICKEN ON COCONUT "CAULI-RICE"/158
CREAMY SIMMERED CHICKEN
WITH OLIVES, SALAMI AND CAPERS/160
PONZU DUCK SALAD
WITH CUCUMBER NOODLES/162
TURKEY CABBAGE WRAPS WITH
CAESAR DRESSING/164
CHICKEN AND COCONUT BROTH/166

CHERMOULA CHICKEN KEBABS
WITH DUKKHA YOGHURT

Chermoula is a brilliant Moroccan marinade that is traditionally used on lamb. You can add it to marinades. dip your bread in it or use it to add a good kick to a stew or casserole. A chermoula recipe is given below but if you don't have that kind of time. an organic pre-packed variety could save you half an hour.

FOR THE CHERMOULA (MAKES 1½ CUPS):
1½ tbsp ground coriander • 2 tbsp ground cumin • 1 heaped tbsp turmeric • ½ tsp dried red chilli
½ tsp coarse salt • 3 tsp paprika • 1½ red onions. minced (about 1 cup)
2 cloves garlic. minced • 1 tbsp tomato paste • 1 handful fresh parsley
1 handful fresh coriander • juice of 2 lemons • 1 cup olive oil
40g roasted cashew nuts

1/ Purée all the ingredients into a fine paste.
2/ Add to a saucepan and cook for about 15 minutes. until the oil and fibre begins to split.
3/ Store in a sterilised jar for up to a month.

FOR THE DUKKHA YOGHURT:
1 cup extra-thick Greek yoghurt • 2 cloves garlic. mashed
¼ cup dukkha (from any supermarket) • salt and pepper

1/ Combine all the ingredients and leave to stand for an hour to infuse.

FOR THE CHICKEN KEBABS:
8 large bamboo skewers. soaked in water • 2 yellow peppers. cut into squares
16 deboned chicken thighs. cut into three • 1½ cups chermoula

1/ Skewer the kebabs with a square of pepper. then a piece of chicken and continue the pattern until you have six pieces of chicken on each skewer.
2/ Pour the chermoula over the chicken and rub it in.
3/ You can grill these straight away but leaving them for a while. or even overnight. will enhance the flavour dramatically.
4/ Cook them on as high a temperature as possible until nice and dark on the outside.
5/ Serve with the dukkha yoghurt on the side.

Note: Fresh coriander and a twist of fresh lime go a long way to freshen this dish up.

SERVES 4

NOT BUTTER CHICKEN

As the name might suggest. this is not a butter chicken curry. Having said that. it is a more appropriate interpretation of the term "butter chicken". It is chicken. And it is cooked in butter. It tastes like butter. which makes it more like butter chicken than butter chicken could ever be. But it is NOT butter chicken.

6 chicken leg quarters • 1 onion. sliced • 250g button mushrooms. cut into quarters
1 head garlic. cut in half down the middle
1 cup chicken stock • 1 cup white wine
1 cup cream • 250g butter • sprig or two of thyme
salt and pepper

1/ Preheat the oven to 140°C.
2/ Lay the onion. mushroom and garlic in a tray.
3/ Press the legs. skin side up. down on the tray. The tray should be tightly packed and have few gaps between the legs.
4/ Push the garlic pieces between the legs.
5/ Pour over the stock. wine and cream.
6/ Place knobs of butter over the top of the chicken. Add the thyme sprigs and season.
7/ Bake in the oven. uncovered. for two hours. When done. the bake should be well coloured (dark brown) and the meat should be falling off the bone.
8/ There will still be a lot of sauce in the tray. which you can either use as gravy or pour over cauli-rice. For those who like a thicker. more gooey sauce. we recommend draining it out of the tray and reducing it in a saucepan until it is much thicker. then adding it back to the chicken and serving it like that.

SERVES 4

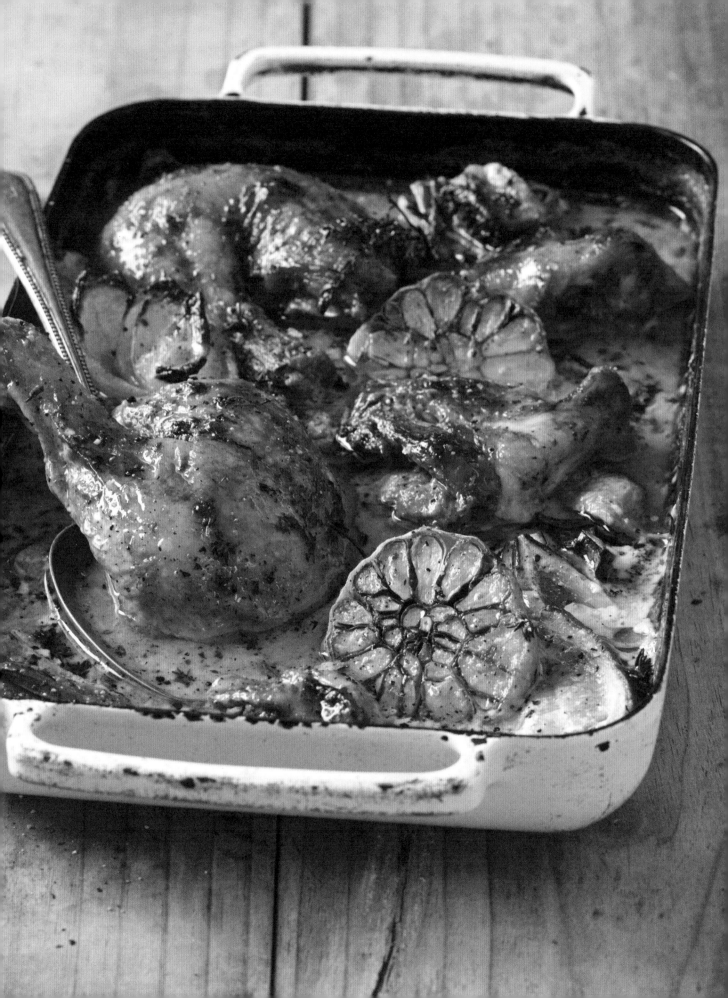

CHICKEN TIKKA MASALA

FOR THE CHICKEN:
500g boneless, skinless chicken thighs • 1 cup extra-thick yoghurt
1 tbsp fresh ginger, grated • 3 cloves garlic, minced • salt and black pepper

1/ Mix the yoghurt, ginger and garlic and season to taste.
2/ Add chicken and marinate for at least 30 minutes.

FOR THE SAUCE:
3 tbsp butter • 2 tsp olive oil • 2 cloves garlic, minced
1½ tbsp ginger, peeled and minced • 1 red chilli, minced (seeds removed if you don't want it spicy)
2 tbsp tomato paste • 2 tsp paprika • 1 tsp garam masala
7 roma tomatoes, diced (or 1 tin chopped peeled tomatoes)
1½ tsp salt • 2 cups water • ½ cup cream
1 handful fresh coriander, roughly chopped

1/ Place a large pan on medium heat, then add the butter and olive oil. When the butter
has melted, add the garlic, ginger and chilli and sauté until lightly browned.
2/ Add the tomato paste and cook until the tomato has darkened in colour, about three minutes.
3/ Add the paprika and garam masala and sauté for another minute.
4/ Add the tomatoes, salt and water. Bring the sauce to a boil, then turn down the
heat to a simmer and cover.
5/ Cook for 20 minutes, take the pan off the heat and allow the sauce to cool for five minutes.
6/ Meanwhile, preheat your grill and cover a roasting tray with foil.
7/ Remove the chicken thigh chunks from the marinade and place on the tray. Place under the grill
and cook for about five minutes on each side, until lightly charred and cooked through. Don't worry
if the chicken is still a little uncooked but charred on the outside – it will cook in the sauce.
8/ Use a blender or food processor to blend the sauce until smooth. Pour back into the pan.
Bring the sauce back up to a boil and add the chicken.
9/ Reduce heat to a simmer and cook, covered, for about 10 minutes.
10/ Add the cream and fresh coriander, stir through and serve.

SERVES 4

PARMESAN CHICKEN PIECES
WITH ROAST GARLIC TOMATO MOLE

FOR THE CHICKEN:
2 large chicken breasts • ½ cup Parmesan, finely grated • ¼ cup almond flour
salt and pepper • 1 egg, beaten • 100g butter

1/ Mix the Parmesan, almond flour and salt and pepper together.
2/ Dunk the breasts in the egg, then into the Parmesan flour, making sure
the coating is nice and thick.
3/ In a heavy-based frying pan, melt the butter on a medium heat and grill the chicken breasts
until golden brown. If they are not cooked through, you can finish them off in the oven (this helps
prevent the crumbs from burning). They shouldn't cook for longer than 10 minutes in total.

FOR THE MOLE:
1 head garlic • 60g butter • 1 tin whole peeled tomatoes • 1 tbsp sweet smoked paprika
1 onion, roughly chopped • 1 handful fresh origanum, roughly chopped • salt and pepper

1/ Preheat the oven to 180˚C.
2/ Cut the top off the garlic and press half the butter into the meat of it.
Wrap it in tinfoil and cook upright in the oven for 45 minutes.
3/ Meanwhile, fry the onion in the rest of the butter in a small pot on a low heat.
Once it's golden brown, add the tinned tomatoes and smoked paprika. Cook on
a low heat for about 10 minutes. If it goes too dry, add a drop or two of water.
4/ Remove the garlic from the oven and squeeze the flesh straight into the sauce.
Add the origanum and heat for a minute or two.
5/ Using a potato masher, mash the tomatoes and garlic together to form a thick,
chunky, smoky tomato sauce.
6/ Season with salt and pepper and serve with the chicken.

Note: You could add a squeeze of lemon to the sauce if it lacks acidity.
If you have made the sauce in advance you could spread it in a small oven dish
and actually finish the chicken off in the oven, on top of the sauce

SERVES 2

CHICKEN LIVERS PERI-PERI

The secret to great livers is to cook them in a fiercely hot pan. The ingredients are very simple but following the steps in the right order is paramount!

250g chicken livers • 1 large onion. sliced • 50g butter
4 cloves garlic. roughly chopped • 2 red chillies. chopped • ½ cup white wine
1 cup tomato purée • juice of 1 large lemon • coconut oil • salt and pepper
1 handful basil. roughly chopped

1/ To make the sauce. sauté the onion in butter on a low heat until soft.
sweet and golden brown. Add the garlic and chilli and sauté until fragrant.
2/ Add the wine and reduce by half. Add the tomato purée and lemon juice and simmer
for a minute. Season to taste with salt and pepper and set aside.
3/ Clean the livers. cut into bite-size pieces and toss them in oil. salt and pepper.
4/ Get a large heavy-based frying pan smoking hot. Drop the livers in the pan and
quickly spread them so they're in one layer. The heat will be quite serious so be careful.
5/ Turn each piece using a fork or lifter. Do not stir them. You want to keep them quite
still in the pan to get great colour and stop them from leaching their juices.
6/ When the livers are nice and brown on each side. pour the sauce into the pan and simmer
for a minute or two.
7/ Season with salt and pepper and add the fresh basil. Check the seasoning one last time
and serve immediately.

Note: It sucks eating chicken livers without a soft floury Portuguese roll but
give it bash on some of the cauliflower mash. you won't be disappointed!

SERVES 2

ROAST CHICKEN

The roast chicken is a staple when eating like William Banting. It gives you everything you need apart from the veggies. If you roast it properly, you get some good fat in the tray for later use. you obviously get heaps of protein but more importantly, once you've finished carving, you can bang that carcass straight into water to make a broth (read more about this in "Basics").

1 free-range chicken • ½ head garlic • 1 tbsp fresh origanum • 1 tbsp fresh thyme.
1 tbsp fresh parsley • salt and pepper • 2 tbsp olive oil • 1 medium onion. halved
3 tbsp butter. softened

1/ Preheat the oven to 200˚C.
2/ Using a pestle and mortar. grind half the garlic and herbs with salt. pepper and olive oil.
3/ Rinse the chicken with cool water. inside and out. Pat dry with paper towel.
4/ Rub the herbed paste all over the chicken. Season with salt and pepper.
5/ Stuff the cavity with half the onion and the remaining garlic and herbs. then
place the chicken. breast-side up. in a roasting pan.
6/ Put the remaining half onion into the pan. which will help colour and flavour the sauce.
Melt the butter and pour over the chicken. Roast for 25 minutes.
7/ Baste the chicken with the drippings and cook for another 25 minutes to brown the skin.
(The legs of the chicken should wiggle easily from the sockets when cooked.)
8/ Transfer the chicken to a platter and allow to stand for 10 minutes so the juices settle
back into the meat before carving.

SERVES 4

GRILLED CHICKEN SALAD
WITH SUNDRIED TOMATOES AND "RANCH DRESSING"

You'll find a Cajun rub recipe below but you can save yourself a few minutes if you get a ready-made one. Just make sure you can pronounce every ingredient listed on the bottle.

FOR THE CAJUN RUB:
1½ tsp yellow mustard seeds • 1 tbsp dried thyme • 1 tsp black pepper
1 tsp cayenne pepper • 1 tsp dried basil • 1 tsp dried origanum
2 tsp paprika (you can use smoked paprika if you want a more smoky flavour)
2 tsp salt

1/ Combine the ingredients and store in a jar.

FOR THE "RANCH DRESSING":
50g blue cheese • 50g cream cheese • 100ml buttermilk • 1 handful parsley, chopped
1 small bunch chives, roughly chopped • salt and pepper • 100ml water

1/ Blend the ingredients in a food processor or with a stick blender.

FOR THE SALAD:
2 chicken breasts • ¼ cup Cajun rub • Splash of olive oil • 2 large handfuls lettuce
1 avocado • ½ cup sundried tomatoes in oil • ¼ cup toasted walnuts • "Ranch dressing"

1/ Place a heavy-based pan over a medium heat.
2/ Rub the chicken with Cajun rub. There should be a thick coating.
3/ Grill the breasts in the pan with a little olive oil. They will blacken a bit but that's fine.
it will give it a charred flavour.
4/ Lower the heat and cover the pan. Leave the breasts to steam on the stove for
a few minutes, then remove from the heat and leave to rest, lid on.
5/ Meanwhile, assemble your salad by spreading out the leaves, topping them with avo,
tomatoes and nuts.
6/ Slice the breasts, pop them onto the salad, smother in dressing and serve.

Note: You could swap the Cajun chicken here for smoked chicken. There are a few good
organic ranch dressings out there but try stay away from artificial emulsifiers.

SERVES 2

ROAST DUCK

1 duck. innards removed • 2 cups chicken stock • salt and pepper
4 tbsp Chinese five spice • garlic. finely chopped

1/ Preheat the oven to 160°C.
2/ Rinse the duck and allow it to sit at room temperature for 20 minutes. Lightly prick the skin without piercing the meat. This allows fat to drain during the cooking process.
3/ Mix together the salt. pepper. garlic and spices and rub over the duck. coating it well.
4/ Place the duck in a deep roasting pan and add the stock. The stock will keep the duck from sticking when it roasts.
5/ Place in the oven and roast for two hours.
6/ Carefully remove the duck from the stock. holding it over the pan to drain. Place it back in the roasting pan.
7/ Turn the oven up to 200°C and roast the duck for another 30 minutes.
8/ Remove from the oven and allow to rest. covered with foil. for 20 minutes.
9/ Serve warm.

SERVES 4

KUNG PAO CHICKEN IN COCONUT "CAULI-RICE"

In most cases with chicken, try use the thighs, because they are much juicier and much more flavoursome. They are however slightly more expensive so feel free to swap for breasts. You'll find a basic recipe for "cauli-rice" in "Basics" but this is a nice Asian adaptation.

FOR THE CHICKEN:
400g boneless, skinless chicken thighs, cut into bite-size pieces
2 tsp tamari sauce (naturally fermented) • 2 tsp Chinese rice wine or dry sherry
1 tsp sesame oil • 2 tbsp oyster sauce • 2 tsp Chinese chilli and garlic paste (preferably hot)
2 spring onions • 4 tbsp water • 1 tsp Szechuan peppercorns (optional)
few drops sesame oil (optional)
4 tbsp cashew nuts, roughly chopped

1/ Combine the tamari sauce, rice wine, sesame oil, oyster sauce, chilli paste, spring onions, water and peppercorns in a bowl and mix.
2/ Add a few drops of sesame oil to a smoking-hot wok.
3/ Seal the chicken off on a high heat until it has good colour and is cooked through.
4/ Pour over the sauce and cook until boiling.
5/ Add the nuts, toss through and serve on a bed of steaming "cauli-rice".

FOR THE COCONUT "CAULI-RICE"
¼ large cauliflower, cut into chunks • ½ tin coconut milk
water • fish sauce

1/ Place the cauliflower in a food processor and pulse until it reaches rice consistency.
The trick here is not to leave it running too long and to do small loads.
In big loads, you will often get a mix of large chunks along with purée.
2/ Place the "rice" in a small pot on the stove, along with the coconut milk
and enough water to just reach the top of the mixture.
3/ Cook, covered, for 20 minutes.
4/ Season with a little fish sauce and then serve this directly from the pot
with the kung pao chicken (or any Asian dish).

Note: If you wanted to add some more love to your "cauli-rice",
you could chop through some spring onions and coriander.

SERVES 2

CREAMY SIMMERED CHICKEN WITH OLIVES, SALAMI AND CAPERS

Simmered chicken breaks the normal rules of sealing and removing the meat,
then cooking the veg in the same pan for the flavour and adding the
meat back later. You literally just drop the meat into the boiling sauce and that's it.

2 chicken breasts, cut into thin strips, skin removed and set aside
1 red onion, sliced • 1 red pepper, sliced • 10 thick slices salami, cut into quarters
80g butter • 2 tbsp capers • ¼ cup green olives • 1 cup stock
1 cup cream • salt and pepper

1/ In a large, heavy-based pan, sauté the onion, pepper, salami and chicken skin
in the butter until slightly brown.
2/ Add the capers, olives and stock and boil until reduced by half.
3/ Add the cream and reduce by a third.
4/ Drop the chicken pieces into the sauce and simmer for two to three minutes.
Season with salt and pepper and serve.

Note: You can do the exact same recipe but swap the cream for good-quality tomatoes
(tinned or fresh). It's very similar to a dish called Chicken Chasseur.

SERVES 2

PONZU DUCK SALAD WITH CUCUMBER NOODLES

Here we talk about "noodles" for the first time. Giving up noodles leaves a lot
to be desired in the way of texture in some of our favourite Asian dishes.
At any Chinese store you can buy a Chinese slicer. You can make
"spaghetti" out of almost any vegetable with it. Here, cucumber is used but
you can experiment with whatever you like. If you can't get a Chinese slicer,
you can use one of those shredder/peelers. Those you can get anywhere.

FOR THE DUCK:
2 duck breasts • 4 tbsp tamari soy sauce (naturally fermented) • salt and white pepper

1/ Using a very sharp knife, score the fat in a crisscross pattern.
2/ Soak the breasts in soy sauce for about 15 minutes. Dry the duck breasts completely
using paper towel and season with salt and pepper.
3/ In a pan, seal the duck breasts on a medium heat, skin-side first. Keep them on the
skin until they have completely rendered, then flip them and continue cooking until they
are medium (about eight to 10 minutes).
4/ Rest them for about three minutes, then slice as thinly as possible.

FOR THE DRESSING:
2 tbsp mirin • 3 tbsp rice vinegar • 1 tbsp tamari soy sauce • juice of 1 lime
¼ tsp toasted sesame oil • 5cm piece ginger, thinly sliced

1/ Combine the ingredients in a bowl.

FOR THE SALAD:
½ daikon radish (or 5 small pink radishes), finely sliced • 2 spring onions, finely sliced
6 mange tout, finely sliced • 3cm piece ginger, finely sliced
finely sliced chilli, to taste • ½ cucumber, shredded or cut on a Chinese slicer
½ handful fresh coriander, chopped

1/ Place all the ingredients in a bowl. Add the duck and the dressing and toss gently.
Serve immediately.

SERVES 2

TURKEY CABBAGE WRAPS
WITH CAESAR DRESSING

We don't eat a great deal of turkey in SA. It doesn't have great fat content but it does keep well in the fridge and makes a great change from all of those chicken snacks. These wraps make use of cabbage leaves instead of tortillas. If you're up for it, the "Basics" chapter has a recipe for real carb-free wraps, which are awesome. If you can get hold of a preservative-free, real Caesar dressing, feel free to use it. If not, find one below.

FOR THE DRESSING:
6 cloves garlic, minced • 1 tbsp Dijon mustard • 1 tbsp vinegar • 2 tbsp mayonnaise
½ cup olive oil • juice of 1 lemon • 2 tbsp anchovy fillets, minced

1/ Blitz all the ingredients using a stick blender. Season to taste with salt and pepper.

FOR THE WRAPS:
600g cooked turkey breast • 4 large cabbage leaves (white or red)
½ cup cream cheese • 2 cups lettuce mix • ½ cup mange tout and spring onions, shredded
½ cup cherry tomatoes, cut into quarters • ½ avocado, sliced
100g dried cranberries • salt and pepper

1/ Blanch the cabbage leaves in boiling water for 30 seconds and pat dry.
2/ Top each leaf with a good dollop of cream cheese, half a cup of lettuce
and 150g of turkey on top.
3/ Sprinkle a tablespoon of shredded vegetables and tomatoes on top of the turkey slices.
Add the avocado and berries, drizzle with Caesar dressing and season with salt and pepper.
4/ Roll the leaves, starting at the edge where you placed the turkey and other ingredients.
5/ Using a serrated knife, cut the wraps in half on the diagonal. Arrange on a plate to serve.

SERVES 4

CHICKEN AND COCONUT BROTH

1.2l chicken broth • 100g mushrooms, sliced (the wilder the better)
2 sticks lemongrass, roughly chopped • 4cm piece ginger, grated
1 red chilli, roughly chopped • 400ml coconut milk • 1 tbsp fish sauce
1 tbsp lime juice, plus wedges to serve • 1 handful fresh coriander, roughly chopped

1/ Bring the broth to a boil in a medium-sized saucepan. Add everything apart
from the coriander to the broth and simmer for 10 to 15 minutes.
You'll be able to taste when all of the flavours have integrated nicely.
2/ Add the coriander and serve immediately.

Note: Thai seasoning comprises sweet, salty, spicy, bitter and sour. Because of the
restriction of sugar, it's left out of the recipe but if you've had a good day, a teaspoon
of palm sugar will electrify this broth. You could also add some shredded chicken to this
to make it more substantial.

SERVES 4

One of the best things about **seafood** is that it's pretty hard to get fish from the sea that isn't organic. The most important thing when buying seafood is to make sure it's from a sustainable source and that the fish you are buying is what your fishmonger says it is. Most of these recipes are quick and simple. If complicated flavours confuse you, you're always safe with fish because 90% of the time, all you need is salt and pepper and you're winning. The other bits and bobs are just for the hell of it.

GAME FISH CEVICHE/170

TROUT CARPACCIO WITH CELERY
AND CUCUMBER PICKLE AND GOAT'S CHEESE/172

BAKED LINEFISH WITH LEMON,
BACON AND TOMATO/174

WARM HADDOCK AND CAULIFLOWER SALAD
WITH TAHINI DRESSING/176

TOM YUM PRAWN BROTH/178

HERRING, CUCUMBER AND FENNEL SALAD
WITH MUSTARD AND CREAM CHEESE DRESSING/180

POACHED FISH ON BUTTERED GREENS/182

SEARED TUNA WITH WARM ITALIAN UMAMI SALAD/184

THAI STEAMED FISH POCKET/186

GRILLED CALAMARI WITH OLIVES
AND CABANOSSI/188

FISH BAKE IN SPICY TOMATO SAUCE/190

GRILLED CHILLI AND GARLIC PRAWNS/192

STEAMED MUSSEL POT/194

FISH SOUP WITH TOMATO AND CHORIZO/196

GAME FISH CEVICHE

By now in our culinary development, most people are used to ordering raw fish from a restaurant, but many are still afraid to make it raw at home. Compared to a restaurant kitchen, your home kitchen will be a lot cleaner and safer than any restaurant kitchen The only word of warning here is that tilefish and swordfish have unusually high mercury content so maybe don't go nuts on these if you're pregnant.

400g raw game fish, filleted, bones out, skin off (yellowtail, tuna, cape salmon, wahoo etc)
100g cherry tomatoes, halved • juice of 2 lemons • Juice of 1 lime
2 tbsp capers, roughly chopped • 1 handful mint, washed and chopped
1 handful dill, washed and chopped • 1 handful coriander, washed and chopped
1 bunch spring onions, finely chopped • lots of salt and pepper • ½ cup extra-virgin olive oil

1/ Combine all ingredients apart from the fish and allow to steep for 20 minutes.
2/ Dice the fish into one-centimetre cubes (you can ask your fishmonger to do this for you).
3/ Cover the fish in marinade and allow to stand for 20 to 25 minutes. The longer you leave it, the more the fish will "cook" in the lemon and lime juice.

Note: Adding avocado to this seriously takes it up a notch.

SERVES 2

TROUT CARPACCIO WITH CELERY
AND CUCUMBER PICKLE AND GOAT'S CHEESE

This is another very light lunch or starter-type dish. The oily trout. creamy and sharp cheese along with the crunchy celery and cucumber pickle create such a great mix of texture in the mouth. The flavours here are seriously fresh and exhilarating.

200g smoked trout ribbons or thinly-sliced raw trout • ¼ cucumber. shaved
2 sticks celery. shaved • juice of 1 lemon • 3 tbsp apple cider vinegar
1 red chilli. finely chopped • 4 tbsp olive oil • 50g chevin (or basic. clean goat's cheese)

1/ Mix together the cucumber. celery. lemon juice. vinegar. chilli and olive oil in a bowl.
2/ Lay the trout ribbons flat on a plate. Top the trout evenly with the celery and cucumber pickle.
3/ Break the goat's cheese into little pieces and dot it around the salad before serving.

Note: Leaving the pickle for about half an hour. if you have the time. really enhances the flavour.

SERVES 2

BAKED LINEFISH WITH LEMON, BACON AND TOMATO

You shouldn't really mess with the flavour of a grilled piece of fish. If you make sure it's fresh, you've won half the battle already. One should be careful not to serve very strong-flavoured accompaniments with the wrong fish as it could be completely overshadowed. You'll be advised when you should use a game fish (much stronger in flavour) or a white fish (like hake or cod).

1kg game fish, skin on, bones removed (preferably yellowtail) • 220g good-quality bacon, sliced
100g butter • 200g cherry tomatoes, halved • zest and juice of 1 large lemon
250ml cream • 1 large handful basil, ripped • 1 cup white wine

1/ Preheat the oven to 140°C.
2/ In a large pan, sauté the bacon in the butter until it begins to crisp. Add the cherry tomatoes and zest and crank the heat up to high – they need to colour a bit.
3/ Add the wine and lemon juice and reduce by half. Add the cream and reduce slightly.
4/ Place the fish in a well-greased oven dish and evenly spoon over the mixture from the pan.
5/ Place in the oven for about 20 minutes. You can tell it is cooked by using a fork in the thickest part of the fillet to pull the meat to the side. If it flakes away nicely and is still moist, you're on the money.
6/ Serve with basil on top.

Note: When cooking fish there are two schools of thought: cook it fast and hot and get lots of colour but risk overcooking it; cook it slowly on a low temp and guarantee a perfect melt-in-the-mouth sensation. Some fancy restaurants cook fish at 70°C and it literally melts.

SERVES 4

WARM HADDOCK AND CAULIFLOWER SALAD WITH TAHINI DRESSING

Smoked haddock is another great item to have on the quick-draw. There are haddock dishes that work with every meal time. but it's not bacon!

FOR THE DRESSING:
4 tbsp tahini • 1 clove garlic. crushed • juice of 1 lemon
1 handful chives. finely chopped • 2 tbsp double thick Greek yoghurt

1/ Combine the ingredients in a small bowl. While whisking continuously. add drops of cold water one tablespoon at a time until you reach the consistency you like (usually about 100ml of water).

FOR THE SALAD:
300g smoked haddock • 100g butter • 300g cauliflower. cut into small pieces
½ cup sliced almonds. toasted

1/ Preheat the oven to 180°C.
2/ Melt the butter in the microwave and drizzle it over the cauliflower in a small tray. Roast the cauliflower until it is golden on the edges. about 30 minutes.
3/ Add the haddock to the tray and leave it in the oven for about 10 minutes.
4/ Remove the tray from the oven. break up the haddock and mix well in a bowl or the tray.
5/ Portion the salad onto plates and scatter with almonds. Drizzle generously with the dressing and serve.

Note: If you've been good with your carbs for the day. this is epic with some pomegranate rubies scattered over it.

SERVES 2

TOM YUM PRAWN BROTH

In the West we use chicken stock but in Laos and Thailand they use stock
from fish bones and prawn shells. Use whichever is easier for you.

2 cups rich broth • 250g (1 cup) prawn tails, shelled and deveined • 1 handful coriander
2 red chillies, halved down the middle • 3 kaffir lime leaves • 1 stick lemongrass, tied in a knot
1 large tomato, cut into wedges • 1 black mushroom, sliced • 1 tbsp hot Thai chilli jam or paste
juice of 1 lime • 1 tbsp fish sauce

1/ With the prawns and coriander set aside, combine all the ingredients
in a pot and bring to a boil.
2/ Simmer for 10 minutes, then add the prawns and coriander.
3/ Balance the seasoning with lime juice and fish sauce and serve.

SERVES 2

HERRING, CUCUMBER AND FENNEL SALAD WITH A MUSTARD AND CREAM CHEESE DRESSING

Pickled herring is seriously underrated, but with its simple flavours,
it's a really diverse delicacy. Herring comes in about a thousand formats
so, honestly, you can use it however you like in this recipe.

FOR THE DRESSING:
1½ tbsp wholegrain mustard • ¼ cup thick cream cheese • juice of 1 lemon
3 tbsp water • ¾ cup milk • 1 handful chives, finely chopped

1/ Combine the ingredients, apart from the chives, in a bowl and blend with a stick blender.
Season with salt and pepper and mix through the chives.

FOR THE SALAD:
200g pickled herring • 100g wild rocket
½ large bulb fennel, finely shaved or sliced (reserve the fronds if you can)
¼ cucumber, peeled or shaved • 1 tomato, cut into wedges • ¾ cup dressing

1/ Lay the rocket on a platter and evenly scatter the fennel, cucumber, tomato and herring over it.
Dress with the mustard dressing and serve immediately.

SERVES 2

POACHED FISH ON BUTTERED GREENS

Poaching is one of the most underrated methods of cooking fish. You are far less likely to dry it out and when using a well-flavoured poaching stock, you have the ability to penetrate the flavour much deeper. Generally, oily fish are much better for poaching (salmon, trout, mackerel, haddock etc).

2 x 180g portions oily fish (salmon, trout, mackerel, haddock, etc) • 1 cup white wine
750ml water • 1 bay leaf • 5 peppercorns • 1 sprig thyme • 1 handful parsley
zest of 1 lemon • 60g fine French beans • 60g mange tout • 50ml cream
2 tbsp capers • 100g butter

1/ Fill a small pot with the wine, water, bay leaf, peppercorns, thyme, parsley and lemon zest. Bring it to a boil, simmer for about five minutes, then reduce the heat to an "almost-bubble".
2/ While the stock is boiling, blanch the beans and mange tout in it and refresh them with cold water or an ice bath.
3/ Drop the fish portions into the stock and leave them for about five minutes. Remove them from the liquid and set aside.
4/ Using a slotted spoon, remove the solids from the water and reduce it to less than a cup. To do this, transfer it to a pan to widen the surface area.
5/ Add the cream and capers and reduce till thick.
6/ Add the butter and fish to the pan, shaking the pan continuously to emulsify the butter.
7/ Add the beans and mange tout, warm through and serve.

SERVES 2

SEARED TUNA WITH WARM ITALIAN UMAMI SALAD

Umami is supposedly the sixth flavour after sweet, sour, salty, spicy and bitter (these make up a lot of Asian flavours). It is the general moreishness you get out of food that contains MSG, soy sauce and a few other things. In fact, Parmesan is classed as the Mediterranean umami. When you think about it, it makes sense! What doesn't taste good with Parmesan on it? Because soy sauce (which marries well with tuna) is kind of a no-no in Banting, the Italian tuna variation below will hopefully give you the same moreishness!

2 x 200g tuna steaks • 3 tbsp good-quality anchovies, minced • zest and juice of 2 lemons
1 cup cherry tomatoes, halved
1 yellow pepper, cut into squares (the size of the cherry tomatoes)
1 tbsp capers, roughly chopped • 1 red onion, sliced • ½ cup olive oil
2 cloves garlic, crushed • 10 basil leaves, shredded • 80g shaved Parmesan

1/ Mix the ground anchovies and lemon zest into a paste and smear it on the tuna steaks.
2/ Combine the lemon juice, tomatoes, pepper, capers, red onion, olive oil, garlic, remaining anchovy and lemon paste and basil in a bowl.
3/ Get a pan smoking hot and sear the tuna for about 45 seconds on each side. If you like it well-done, by all means, let it go longer.
4/ Once the tuna is cooked, remove it from the pan and immediately add the mixture from the bowl, letting it simmer, spit and boil for about two minutes. All of those flavours will come out beautifully.
5/ Place the tuna on the plate and spoon over the warm salad. Top with Parmesan shavings and serve immediately.

Note: If anchovies aren't your game, feel free to leave them out. They also add to the umami but for a lot of people, they're a bit much.

SERVES 2

THAI STEAMED FISH POCKET

A fish pocket is quite similar to poaching in that you are able to penetrate the fish with flavour. You're also not bound to the indoor kitchen with pockets as they cook just as well directly on hot coals as they do in the oven.

2 x 200g portions white fish (hake, cod, cob etc) • 200ml coconut cream
2 limes • 2 tbsp fish sauce • 1 tbsp Thai chilli and garlic sauce • 1 tsp red curry paste
2 spring onions, finely chopped • 1 handful fresh coriander, roughly chopped
2 small heads bok choi, halved lengthways

1/ In a bowl, combine everything apart from the bok choi and the fish.
2/ Lay out two large sheets of heavy-duty foil, then lay two sheets of greaseproof paper on top of those.
In the centre of each sheet, place two pieces of bok choi.
Place a fish portion on top of each one and raise the edges of the foil to create a bowl.
3/ Pour half of the sauce into each "bowl", then scrunch the sides together to close the pocket.
4/ Place the pocket directly on the coals for eight minutes or in the oven at 200°C for 12 minutes.
5/ To serve, plate the fish and pour over the sauce from the pocket.

Note: You can use the same sauce pocket recipe with prawns or mussels.

SERVES 2

GRILLED CALAMARI WITH OLIVES AND CABANOSSI

If you can get clean baby calamari, this dish can be finished in 10 minutes!

560g baby calamari tubes and tentacles • 200g cabanossi, sliced • 2 red peppers, finely diced
1 cup marinated green or black olives • 4 cloves garlic, minced • 1 bunch flat-leaf parsley, chopped
juice of 1 lemon • salt and pepper

1/ In a large heavy-based pan, sauté the cabanossi and olives on a medium heat until crispy.
Remove the olives and cabanossi but leave the oil in the pan.
2/ Pump the heat up to full and wait for it to get smoking hot. Add the peppers and give it
a quick stir, then quickly add the calamari and leave for a minute or so to colour. Do not stir.
3/ After a minute, you can move it around a little and toss the tubes. Once the tubes begin
colouring, add the garlic, olives and cabanossi and toss again.
4/ Add the parsley and lemon juice and season with salt and pepper.

Note: You could also add a small knob of butter at the end; it would bring it together brilliantly.

SERVES 4

FISH BAKE IN SPICY TOMATO SAUCE

This recipe calls for salted lemon in the ingredients. You could just as well use normal lemon zest but you'll find a nice recipe for salted lemon below. The salt pickles the lemons, giving them a lot more depth and flavour.

FOR THE SALTED LEMONS:
6 lemons • 250g coarse salt • 1 tbsp black peppercorns • 4 bay leaves

1/ Cut the lemons almost into quarters (like a deep crisscross, leaving a centimetre still attached at the bottom).
2/ Pack as much salt as possible into the heart of each lemon.
3/ Layer the lemons, peppercorns and bay leaves in a jar. Force them into as small a jar as possible and close with a lid.
4/ Leave for at least two weeks.

FOR THE FISH BAKE:
8 x 200g portions of any white fish • salt and pepper • olive oil • 50g butter
2 tsp harissa paste • 10 pitted olives (green, black or mixed) • 2 anchovy fillets
2 tbsp lemon zest, finely shaved • ½ tsp paprika • 2 cups tomato, chopped and seeded
1 cup onions, chopped • 2 tbsp minced garlic • ¼ cup parsley, roughly chopped
2 tbsp fresh origanum • 1 tbsp fresh thyme

1/ Preheat the oven to 200°C.
2/ Season both sides of the fish with salt, pepper and olive oil.
3/ To make the sauce, sauté the onions in butter until golden. Add the garlic and sauté until fragrant, then add the remaining ingredients and simmer for five minutes on a low heat.
4/ Pack the fish pieces tightly in a lasagne or baking dish and cover with the sauce. Bake for about 40 minutes, basting occasionally with the pan juices.
5/ Remove from the oven and allow to rest for 15 minutes. Top with some fresh herbs for garnish.

SERVES 8

GRILLED CHILLI AND GARLIC PRAWNS

FOR THE SAUCE:
2 red chillies, very finely chopped • 5 cloves garlic, crushed
¾ cup olive oil • ¼ cup lemon juice, with the zest of each lemon

1/ Combine all of the ingredients in a small saucepan and simmer for five minutes.

FOR THE PRAWNS:
24 large prawns • 200g butter • olive oil • 2 tsp crushed garlic • 2 tbsp lemon juice
2 tbsp hot chilli sauce or chopped chilli • salt and black pepper

1/ In a massive frying pan, heat the butter and a bit of olive oil before adding the garlic, lemon
juice and chilli. Sauté for a minute are two to let the flavours come out, then add the prawns.
2/ Sauté the prawns for four to five minutes, turning, until cooked.
3/ Use tongs to transfer the prawns from the pan into a warm serving dish.
4/ Add the sauce to the pan, season and mix well with the bits left in the pan from the prawns.
Bring to a boil and simmer for a minute or so before tipping the sauce over the prawns.
5/ Serve immediately.

Note: Add a massive handful of freshly chopped parsley to this for a whack of freshness.

SERVES 4

STEAMED MUSSEL POT

In South Africa, this is an absolute classic. It is usually cooked in a cast iron pot on the coals, but you can do it in anything you like.

1.5kg black mussels • ¼ cup olive oil • 3 tbsp butter • 1 medium onion, finely chopped
4 garlic cloves, minced • 2 sticks celery, finely chopped. • ¼ bunch fresh thyme
1 cup white wine • 200ml cream • 1 handful basil, roughly chopped

1/ Rinse the mussels under cold running water. Remove the stringy mussel beards and discard any open mussels or those with broken shells.
2/ Heat the olive oil and 3 tbsp of butter in a large pot over medium heat. Add the onion, garlic, celery and thyme and cook for about five minutes.
3/ Add the white wine and bring to the boil. Add the cream, bring to the boil again and add the mussels.
4/ Close the pot with a lid and steam over medium-high heat for 10 minutes, until the mussels open. Stir occasionally so that all the mussels are in contact with the heat.
5/ Season with salt and pepper, sprinkle with basil and serve immediately.

SERVES 4

FISH SOUP WITH TOMATO AND CHORIZO

1 chorizo sausage, sliced • 2 tbsp olive oil • 1 large onion, finely chopped
2 tbsp garlic, minced • 1 stick lemongrass, finely chopped
4 sticks celery, finely diced • ½ cup white wine • 1 tin chopped peeled tomatoes
4 cups fish or chicken stock • 600g fresh fish, diced
½ cup parsley, finely chopped • juice of 1 lemon

1/ In a large saucepan, heat the olive oil and sauté the chorizo for three to four minutes.
2/ Add the onion, garlic, lemongrass and celery and continue sautéing for three minutes.
3/ Add the wine and reduce by half. Stir in the tomatoes and stock and simmer for 10 minutes.
4/ Add the fish and simmer for another five minutes (or until the fish is cooked).
5/ Stir in the chopped parsley, season to taste with salt, pepper and lemon juice
and serve immediately.

SERVES 4

Sides & Salads

Contrary to popular belief, vegetables still make up the largest part of Banting. A lot of people think Banting is just fat and meat but that's hogwash. The reason we shamelessly promote this life is because the benefits of eating so many nutritious, low-carb veggies by far outweighs the benefits of eating rice and potatoes at every meal.

You'll find a decent mix of quick, medium and slightly slower recipes for veggies. There are thousands of veggies out there so please don't use this as your strict guide. Swap ingredients in and out and match different sides with different meat and fish dishes. There are two golden rules to follow when planning a menu that you may find helpful.
1. Always make sure that, across the menu, you have a good mix of flavours that go well together.
2. Keep in mind the textures that each dish or element will offer. To keep things exciting you always want to have a little crunch, something smooth or creamy and then something that offers a little more chew like a protein. If you're serving mashed cauliflower, the last thing you would pair it with would be mushy aubergines. You would want to go with some crunchy broccoli or al dente asparagus.

If you're trying a completely new vegetable and aren't sure what to do with it, always start by adding butter and bacon, and see how you go from there.

ASPARAGUS, PARMESAN, LEMON AND OLIVE OIL/200

COURGETTE AND GARLIC GRATIN/202

BUTTERED BRUSSELS SPROUTS WITH BACON AND CRÉME FRAÎCHE/204

WILTED ONION AND WALNUT SPINACH/206

SHIITAKE MUSHROOM, BOK CHOI AND MANGE TOUT STIR-FRY/208

GREEN BEANS WITH TOASTED ALMONDS AND LEMON BUTTER/210

CRUNCHY CABBAGE SALAD WITH CREAMY RED CURRY DRESSING/212

BROCCOLI AND AVOCADO SALAD WITH ROASTED ALMOND DRESSING/214

GRILLED PEPPERS, ROCKET, OLIVES AND MOZZARELLA/216

GRILLED ROASTED LEEKS/218

SAGE AND BLUE CHEESE ROASTED GEM SQUASH/220

AVOCADO, SNOW PEA AND MINT SALAD WITH POPPY SEED DRESSING/222

MARINATED TOMATO AND ANCHOVY SALAD/224

SPICED PUMPKIN AND GOAT'S CHEESE, SUNFLOWER SEEDS AND CITRUS DRESSING/226

ASPARAGUS, PARMESAN, LEMON AND OLIVE OIL

Asparagus has such good flavour that we don't dare mess with it.
This dish (and asparagus in general) goes brilliantly with beef, lamb and
fish and does pretty well on its own.

300g thick asparagus spears, corky bases removed • juice of 1 large lemon
40g Parmesan • 50ml extra-virgin olive oil • salt and black pepper

1/ In a small pot, bring some water to a boil. Blanch the asparagus in the water for two minutes
(or until they go bright green), then refresh them in cold water until cooled properly.
2/ Lay them out on plates or a platter and squeeze over some lemon juice.
3/ Shave or grate the Parmesan on top of the asparagus, being sure to coat it well.
4/ Splash with olive oil, season liberally with salt and pepper and serve.

Note: The success of this recipe lies in the freshness and quality of Parmesan.
No other cheese will cut it!

SERVES 2

COURGETTE AND GARLIC GRATIN

This is serious comfort food. It takes no time to prepare and stays in the oven for quite a while so you can bang it in and forget about it.

800g courgettes • 1 onion, roughly sliced • 1 handful thyme sprigs
1 head garlic, cloves peeled • 250ml cream • 100g butter, broken into pieces
salt and pepper

1/ Preheat the oven to 150˚C.
2/ Cut the courgettes into quarters down the middle.
3/ Lay the onion, courgettes, thyme and garlic in a lasagne or casserole dish.
Season, mix well and then press down.
4/ Dot butter over the top of the dish and cover with cream.
5/ Place in the oven, uncovered, for approximately one and a half hours. Serve hot.

Note: If you want some extra goodness, before you serve it, give it a layer of grated cheese on top and pop it back under the grill for a cheesy crust.

SERVES 4

BUTTERED BRUSSELS SPROUTS
WITH BACON AND CRÈME FRAÎCHE

For those who are not huge Brussels sprouts fans, you'd be surprised at how
the bacon and butter formula can release a new side to these nutrient-packed veggies.
Kind of like the ugly duckling and the swan.

500g Brussels sprouts • 120g streaky bacon, cut into lardons • 40g butter
100g double thick crème fraîche • salt and pepper

1/ In a small pot, steam the Brussels sprouts until soft.
2/ In a heavy-based pan, sauté the bacon in the butter until it begins to crisp.
3/ Add the Brussels sprouts and toss them in the bacon and butter to give them a good coating.
Season to taste.
4/ Keep cooking until the sprouts are warmed through.
5/ Serve immediately garnished with dollops of crème fraîche over the sprouts.

Note: You can convert this recipe to a bake by adding cream and leaving it
on a tray in the oven at 180°C for about an hour.

SERVES 4

WILTED ONION AND WALNUT SPINACH

This is actually a filling for a Middle-Eastern pastry called fatayer. little pastry triangles that get served at all special occasions. especially in Lebanon. You could serve this with pretty much anything or eat it on its own.

200g Swiss chard or baby spinach. washed and roughly chopped • 1 large onion. roughly chopped 40g butter • ½ tsp sumac (optional) • juice of one lemon • ⅓ cup walnuts. chopped and toasted 1 small bunch mint. finely chopped • salt and pepper

1/ In a medium-sized pot. gently sauté the onion in butter until translucent.
2/ Add the spinach and continue to stir until the spinach has cooked and any excess juice has evaporated.
3/ Add the sumac (if desired). a squeeze of lemon. the nuts and mint and stir well.
4/ Season to taste and serve immediately or set aside for later.

SERVES 2

SHIITAKE MUSHROOM, BOK CHOI
AND MANGE TOUT STIR-FRY

1 tbsp coconut oil • 2 cloves garlic, minced • 5cm piece ginger, peeled and grated or julienned
1 small chilli, minced • 1 bunch spring onion, finely sliced • 150g fresh shiitake mushrooms, sliced
200g mange tout, halved lengthways • 200g baby bok choi, thickly sliced
1 tbsp fish sauce • 2 tbsp mirin • juice of 1 lime • 1 large handful basil, roughly chopped
2 tbsp sesame seeds, toasted

1/ In a wok, heat the coconut oil over a high heat.
2/ As the oil begins to smoke, add the garlic, ginger, chilli and spring onion and mix.
3/ Before the garlic starts to colour, add the mushrooms and sauté them for about
two minutes. Once they are cooked, add the mange tout and sauté until bright green.
4/ Add the bok choi and cook until wilted.
5/ Season with fish sauce, mirin and lime juice. Mix through the basil leaves
and sesame seeds and serve.

SERVES 4

GREEN BEANS WITH TOASTED ALMONDS AND LEMON BUTTER

Green beans and almonds is a classic French combination used as a side
in a lot of restaurants. These pair pretty well with anything simple like
a grilled piece of meat or fish.

400g green beans. topped and tailed • 60g butter • 3 tbsp almond slithers. toasted in a dry pan
juice of 1 lemon • salt and pepper

1/ In a small pot. bring some water to a boil and blanch the beans for two minutes.
Refresh them in cold or iced water so they keep their colour and texture.
2/ In a large pan or wok. melt the butter and warm it until just before it turns brown.
then add the beans. (If the butter is a little brown. it will add a nice nutty flavour.)
3/ Toss the beans until they are warmed through. then add the almonds and lemon juice.
4/ Season with salt and pepper and serve.

SERVES 4

CRUNCHY CABBAGE SALAD WITH CREAMY RED CURRY DRESSING

Cabbage is one of the most underrated salad leaves out there. It's dirt cheap and packed with tangy peppery flavour. This recipe strays from the standard coleslaw to show how cabbage holds its own against much more exciting flavours.

FOR THE DRESSING:
1 tbsp good-quality red Thai curry paste • 1 tbsp lime juice • 1 tbsp fish sauce
150ml coconut cream • 2 tbsp macadamia nut butter
1 handful fresh coriander, roughly chopped

1/ Place all the ingredients in a small saucepan and bring to the boil. Set aside and leave to cool.

FOR THE SALAD:
½ white cabbage, shredded • 1½ cups bean sprouts • 1 bunch spring onions
1 cup toasted macadamia nuts (other nuts will be okay, just keep an eye on the carbs)

1/ Combine all the ingredients in a mixing bowl and cover in dressing.
Mix everything together and serve immediately.

Note: In Thailand, they don't generally use salt and pepper. Traditionally they season with lime juice (acidity), fish sauce (salty) and palm sugar (sweetness), so if you don't have lime juice or fish sauce you could always just add a squeeze of lemon and some salt to get the flavour right.

SERVES 4

BROCCOLI AND AVOCADO SALAD WITH ROASTED ALMOND DRESSING

This is another very simple yet delicious creamy salad recipe.

FOR THE DRESSING:
½ cup whole almonds • 1 tbsp lemon juice • 1 tbsp wholegrain mustard
4 tbsp crème fraîche • 100ml milk

1/ Roast the nuts in the oven at 180°C or under the grill until they are golden brown,
then chop them up roughly.
2/ Add the remaining ingredients and half the nuts to a tall, narrow container
and blend using a stick blender.
3/ Stir in the remaining nuts and season to taste.

Note: We blend only half the nuts because they help make the dressing creamy and the flavour
infuses better that way. The second addition of crushed nuts is for a crunchy texture.

FOR THE SALAD:
400g tenderstem broccoli (you could use normal broccoli, broken up into florets)
2 ripe avocados, pitted and cut into chunks • 1 bunch spring onion, finely sliced
1 small packet wild rocket

1/ In a small pot of boiling salted water, blanch the broccoli until al dente (still crunchy)
and refresh it in cold water.
2/ Combine the broccoli, avocados, spring onion and wild rocket, mix gently
and spread over a platter.
3/ Pour over the dressing and serve.

Note: Just make sure the dressing has cooled before pouring it over the salad
as it may cause the avocado to discolour.

SERVES 4

GRILLED PEPPERS, ROCKET, OLIVES AND MOZZARELLA

This is a brilliant salad with lamb or game fish and also acts as a nice alternative to the standard caprese salad. Just like the caprese, the quality of the mozzarella you use will make a huge impact on the end result.

1 large ripe red pepper • 1 large ripe yellow pepper • 30ml red wine vinegar
100ml extra-virgin olive oil • 1 clove garlic • 2 sprigs thyme
1 small bag rocket • 1 ball buffalo mozzarella, broken into chunks
¼ cup marinated olives

1/ Char the peppers directly on the gas hob until they are pitch black all over.
Seal them in an airtight container and leave them to sweat until cool
(this helps separate the skin from the flesh).
2/ Remove the peppers and use a knife to scrape the skin off the outside and the seeds out the inside.
3/ Cut each pepper into four equal sized "fillets".
4/ Add the peppers, red wine vinegar, olive oil, garlic and thyme to a small saucepan and bring to a simmer for about five minutes for the flavours to infuse and get sucked up by the peppers.
5/ Once the peppers have cooled, lay them on a flat platter and top with mozzarella chunks, olives and rocket.
6/ Drizzle the remaining dressing over the leaves and serve immediately.

Note: You can also make this salad on a fire by placing the peppers directly onto the coals until black and then following the remaining steps.

SERVES 2

GRILLED ROASTED LEEKS

400g baby leeks • olive oil for basting
100g butter • 10 sprigs thyme • salt and pepper

1/ Preheat the oven to 200°C.
2/ Blanch the leeks. whole. in salted water until soft. then refresh in cold water.
3/ Get a griddle pan smoking hot.
4/ Baste the leeks with oil to give them a good coating. then grill them on the griddle
until they are nicely charred.
5/ Place them in a roasting tray and cover with thyme. salt and pepper and chunks of butter.
6/ Roast them in the oven until they are golden brown (roughly 15 minutes) and serve.

Note: These leeks go brilliantly with a good Sunday roast.

SERVES 4

SAGE AND BLUE CHEESE ROASTED GEM SQUASH

4 gem squash, cut in half, seeds removed • 150g blue cheese
1 handful sage leaves • 100g butter

1/ Steam or boil the squash until it is soft and tender.
2/ Remove from the water and place in a tray.
3/ Crumble the blue cheese over each squash.
4/ Melt the butter in a pan and gently fry the sage until it turns golden.
5/ Spoon the butter over each squash and grill in the oven until the cheese is dark brown.

SERVES 4

AVOCADO, SNOW PEA AND MINT SALAD WITH POPPY SEED DRESSING

FOR THE DRESSING:
juice of 1 lemon (25ml) • 2 tbsp red wine vinegar • 1 tsp Dijon mustard
1 clove garlic, minced • 4 tbsp poppy seeds, toasted • 150ml extra-virgin olive oil
salt and pepper

1/ Combine the lemon juice, vinegar, mustard, garlic and poppy seeds in a mixing bowl.
While whisking continuously, pour in the olive oil until a dressing is formed. Season to taste.

FOR THE SALAD:
1 large ripe avocado, cut into chunks • 200g snow peas (sugar snaps or mange tout)
1 bunch spring onion, thinly sliced • 1 head butter lettuce, washed and torn
1 handful of mint leaves

1/ Cut the sugar snaps in half lengthways on the diagonal.
2/ Lay the lettuce leaves out on a platter. Layer with snow peas, avocado, mint and spring onions
and cover with the dressing. Serve immediately.

Note: To give this salad more of a crunch, feel free to add any nut or seed.

SERVES 2

MARINATED TOMATO
AND ANCHOVY SALAD

These tomatoes go very well with pretty much anything.
The anchovy and caper combo goes perfectly on top of carpaccio
or baked fish but you can serve them just like this as a salad.

FOR THE DRESSING:
juice of 1 lemon · 1 cup extra-virgin olive oil · 4 cloves garlic
1 huge bunch Italian parsley, washed · ¼ cup capers, rinsed
80g (1 small tin) anchovies (the best you can find)

1/ Combine all the ingredients and blend with a stick blender.

FOR THE SALAD:
2 heads frisée lettuce, washed · 150g cherry tomatoes, halved
6 roma tomatoes, cut into quarters · 150g yellow cherry tomatoes, halved

1/ Place the tomatoes in a bowl and cover with the dressing.
Leave them in the fridge, covered, for 12 hours or overnight.
2/ Lay the leaves out on a platter and cover them with the tomatoes and the rest of the sauce.

Note: The different tomatoes are in there for colour and texture but you can
just as well use 600g of the same tomato and get a similar result.

SERVES 4

SPICED PUMPKIN AND GOAT'S CHEESE, SUNFLOWER SEEDS AND CITRUS DRESSING

Roasted pumpkin and any cheese is a match made in heaven. You can mix it with stronger flavoured cheeses like chevin, blue cheese or hard cheeses like pecorino and Parmesan but it stands up well to anything. Spices don't go particularly well with blue cheese or pecorino so this recipe uses chevin.

FOR THE DRESSING:
juice of 2 lemons (50ml) • 1 tbsp Dijon mustard • 150ml extra-virgin olive oil
salt and pepper

1/ Combine the lemon juice and mustard in a mixing bowl. While whisking continuously, pour in the olive oil until a dressing is formed. Season to taste.

FOR THE SALAD:
600g pumpkin cubes • olive oil for roasting • 1 tbsp ground cumin
1 tbsp ground coriander • 1 tsp ground nutmeg • salt and pepper
200g chevin, broken into small chunks • ¼ cup sunflower seeds
100g rocket, washed

1/ Preheat the oven to 180˚C.
2/ Toss the pumpkin in oil, cumin, coriander, nutmeg, salt and pepper and place on a tray in the oven until roasted and nicely coloured on the edges (about 45 minutes). Set aside to cool.
3/ Lay the rocket on a platter and top with the pumpkin. Layer chunks of chevin, sunflower seeds and, finally, a liberal splash of dressing.

SERVES 4

Entertaining is by far the hardest hurdle to get over when you change the way you eat, even if it's not Paleo or Banting. You are subjecting your "normal-eating" friends to your preferences and are most likely opening yourself up to criticism. It's while entertaining at a home event when one might succumb to the easy way out and start piling on the bread and dips. Of course, you'd be completely forgiven because, if not bread and dips, what are people supposed to snack on?

Once a drink or two have gone down, keeping your hands out of the "cookie jar" will become almost impossible. In the morning you could wake up having drunk a loaf of bread in beer and on top of that, eaten half a real loaf with dips and pâtés. The well-known Sunday morning "Ah-I-made-a-fool-of-myself-and-can't-believe-I-ate-all-that-rubbish" feeling often leads to an additional day of binging (while you're on a roll, so to speak), which we call Sulking-Sunday. Sulking Sunday often ends at the beginning of Mad Monday, where life is too busy to start Banting again, which then lands one on Suicide Tuesday. Suicide Tuesday is when reality hits home and you realise how far off the wagon you are, and you plan to start from scratch on Wednesday.

Throwing a party or having a get-together should be pure enjoyment, and in no way involve the stress of self-restraint. You don't even need to tell your friends that everything is Banting or Paleo, just serve them delicious food and if they ask, tell them it's good, healthy food.

This chapter works slightly differently to the others. When you entertain, you're likely to mix and match cold meats, dips, crudités and nibbles in a number of different ways. For this reason, everything in this chapter can

be matched with one another. There are guidelines but in all honesty, just have fun. That's what entertaining should be!

NUTTY CRACKERS/230
ROASTED COURGETTE HUMMUS/232
HOT SMOKED FISH PÂTÉ/234
SPICY BACON NUTS/236
PAN-FRIED CHORIZO AND OLIVES/238
CLASSIC CARPACCIO/240
LAMB KOFTA WITH TZATZIKI/242
GRILLED SMOKY HALLOUMI/244
SPICY CHICKEN WINGS
WITH BLUE CHEESE DIP/246
COCONUT-CRUMBED WHITE FISH
WITH CURRY MAYO/248
CHARRED AUBERGINES WITH POMEGRANATE AND TAHINI/250
GRILLED MARINATED VEGGIES/252

NUTTY CRACKERS

Seed crackers are the perfect alternative to your standard bread crackers. There are some never-seen-before ingredients here but don't stress, you can get them from any health shop. These also keep very well in a sealed container.

200g sunflower seeds • 60g flax seeds • 100g sesame seeds
2 tbsp psyllium husks • 500ml water • 1 tsp salt

1/ Preheat the oven to 160°C.
2/ In a mixing bowl, combine all the ingredients and leave the mixture to stand until it is thick and pliable, about 10 minutes.
3/ Spread the mixture out as thinly as possible on a silicone mat on a baking tray (you may need two). The mix should have no holes in it.
4/ Bake the trays for an hour. You may need to rotate them away from the hot spots in the oven.
5/ After an hour and a few turns, it should only take another 15 to 20 minutes until they are seriously crispy.
6/ Remove them from the oven and leave to cool. Once cooled, break them into any size you like and store in an airtight container.

Note: These would go perfectly with any of the pâtés or dips. Blow your mind with a nutty cracker with a thick layer of liver pâté and some charcuterie.

Makes 16 crackers

ROASTED COURGETTE HUMMUS

Although chickpeas aren't true carbs. they are quite high in starch. which puts them close to the red list. Using a basic hummus recipe. you can actually swap the chickpeas for quite a few other veggies (pumpkin. butternut. aubergine. courgette. sundried tomatoes etc.) and get a similar. if not better. result.

500g courgettes. cut into chunks • oil for roasting • ¼ cup fresh lemon juice
¼ cup tahini • 2 cloves garlic. whole • 4 tbsp olive oil
½ tsp kosher salt. depending on taste • ½ tbsp ground cumin

1/ Preheat the oven to 180˚C.
2/ Toss the veg in a light coating of oil. salt and pepper
and roast in the oven until golden brown and mushy.
3/ Place the roasted veg in a food processor along with the remaining ingredients
and purée until smooth.
4/ Leave to infuse for an hour and serve with anything you like.

MAKES 500g

HOT SMOKED FISH PÂTÉ

In South Africa. fish pâté is a staple at any gathering. We use a very bony fish called snoek which has rich and oily meat and is excellent smoked. For this recipe you can use any smoked. rich. oily fish as long as it is fresh!

250g hot smoked fish (snoek. cape salmon. mackerel etc) • 1 large onion. diced
2 cloves garlic. minced • 100g cream cheese • 100g crème fraîche
50g butter • 1 handful Italian parsley. roughly chopped
1 tsp paprika • ½ tsp cayenne pepper • juice of 1 lemon

1/ In a small saucepan. simmer the onion and the garlic in butter until soft
and translucent and fragrant. then remove from the heat to cool.
2/ In a food processor. blend the fish. cream cheese and crème fraîche until smooth.
Tip out into a bowl.
3/ Add the remaining ingredients and leave to stand for an hour or so to infuse.

MAKES 500G

SPICY BACON NUTS

Normal mixed nuts actually make for one of the best Banting snacks.
This is just taking it to the next level.

250g streaky bacon rashers
4 cups assorted nuts (almonds, hazelnuts, pecan, Brazil, macadamia and cashew nuts)
½ tsp ground cumin • ¼ tsp cayenne pepper • 1 large pinch ground nutmeg
2 tsp unsalted butter • 1 tsp salt

1/ Grill the bacon in the oven in a greased oven tray until crispy.
2/ Remove from the fat and cut the rashers into small lardons. Reserve the fat.
3/ Toast the nuts in a large, heavy-based dry pan until golden.
4/ Add the bacon fat and butter and cook until the nuts begin to darken.
5/ Add the spices and fry them in the butter until they become fragrant.
6/ Add a few drops of water and the bacon and toss.
7/ Tip the nuts back onto an oven tray lined with paper towel and pop them
in the oven for another five minutes at 160°C to dry out properly.
8/ Store in an airtight container.

Note: If you keep a permanent supply of these in the cupboard, you could also use them
to add some smack to any dull salad you might find yourself eating.

MAKES 800G

PAN-FRIED CHORIZO AND OLIVES

This classic Spanish snack is probably the quickest dish in the book, but by no means the least exciting. Chorizo gets added to many other recipes to add flavour but sometimes it's nice to just eat it as chorizo.

220g chorizo (1 "horse shoe") • 1 cup great-quality marinated green olives

1/ In a large, heavy-based frying pan, use a tablespoon of the olives' oil to sauté the chorizo on a high heat.
2/ As it begins to caramelise, add the olives.
3/ Sauté them until the olives have some good colour and the chorizo is nicely grilled.
4/ You can serve this hot or cold.

Note: These are a great addition to a meat or cheese platter.
The crispy chorizo also goes particularly well with Banting mayo.

CLASSIC CARPACCIO

If you're entertaining, carpaccio is a perfect dish to prep in advance. Simply follow the steps, slice it onto a platter and keep it covered in the fridge until service time.

400g beef fillet • Crystal salt and black pepper • 2 large lemons
80g Parmesan, finely grated • 4 tbsp capers, drained
30g wild rocket • olive oil

1/ Season the fillet liberally with salt and pepper.
2/ In a smoking-hot pan, grill the fillet just enough to give it a little colour on each side, then cool quickly.
3/ Slice the beef as thin as possible (use a meat slicer if you have one) and lay each slice slightly overlapping the next on a large platter (if you're serving it later, you can pop it into the fridge now).
4/ Generously squeeze lemon juice over the meat. Season it very well with Maldon salt and cracked black pepper.
5/ Evenly scatter with grated Parmesan and capers, top with rocket and a liberal sprinkling of olive oil.

Note: You can swap the beef fillet for fresh tuna or another game fish.

SERVES 4

LAMB KOFTA WITH TZATZIKI

FOR THE KOFTA:

800g lamb mince • 1 onion. chopped • 2 cloves garlic. crushed
olive oil • 1 tbsp ground coriander • 1 tsp salt • 1 tsp ground cumin
½ tsp ground cinnamon • ½ tsp ground allspice • ¼ tsp cayenne pepper • ¼ tsp ground ginger
3 tbsp fresh parsley. chopped • salt and black pepper

1/ Sauté the onion and garlic in oil until softened. Add the salt and spices
and toast them until they become aromatic. Remove from the heat.
2/ Mix the pan contents. the parsley and mince together in a bowl and season well.
3/ Divide the meat mixture into about 14 rough balls. Mould each piece around the pointed
end of a bamboo kebab skewer. making a six-centimetre oval kebab that comes to a point.
just covering the tip of the skewer. Cover and refrigerate for at least one hour before grilling.
4/ Heat a griddle pan over medium heat or prepare a braai.
5/ Brush the meat lightly with olive oil and grill. turning until brown all over
and just cooked through (about five minutes). Serve with tzatziki.

FOR THE TZATZIKI (GREEK CUCUMBER YOGHURT SAUCE):

2 cups double thick Greek yoghurt • 1 medium cucumber. peeled. halved and seeded
2 tsp salt • ½ clove garlic • 1 tbsp olive oil • 1 tbsp lemon juice
½ tbsp fresh mint. finely chopped

1/ Grate the cucumber into a bowl and sprinkle with salt. rubbing it into the cucumber
with your hands. Rest for 20 minutes. then squeeze the cucumbers to release as
much liquid as possible.
2/ Stir the cucumber. garlic. olive oil. lemon juice and mint into the yoghurt. Refrigerate
for at least one hour before serving.

Note: When using wooden skewers be sure to soak them
in water for at least 15 minutes before using them.

SERVES 4

GRILLED SMOKY HALLOUMI

This is a VERY quick and easy snack to serve and you could
serve it with anything from pesto to roast garlic mayo.

FOR THE HOT SMOKY RUB:
1 tsp cumin • 1 tsp smoked paprika • 1 tsp yellow mustard seeds
1 tsp dried thyme • 1 tsp dried origanum
¼ tsp cayenne pepper • ½ tsp salt • 1 tsp ground black pepper

1/ Combine all the ingredients in a bowl.

FOR THE HALLOUMI:
1 batch hot smoky rub • 400g halloumi. cut into 8mm-thick slices • ½ cup olive oil

1/ Place a griddle pan on the heat and warm it until smoking.
2/ Combine the rub and olive oil. then toss with halloumi.
3/ Grill each piece of cheese on the griddle pan for about one minute per side.
They should char on the outside but just about hold their shape. Serve immediately.

Note: If you are doing a huge batch of these. you can lay them on a tray
and warm them all under the grill in the oven just before you serve.

SPICY CHICKEN WINGS WITH BLUE CHEESE DIP

One of the world's most popular bar snacks must be "Buffalo Wings".
Most of the time, chicken wings are drenched in tangy marinade and laced
with sugar for those crispy sticky burnt bits. Here is a sugar-free version
that guarantees the same satisfaction.

FOR THE BLUE CHEESE DIPPING SAUCE:
50g blue cheese (stilton, gorgonzola, roquefort etc) • 50g cream cheese • 200ml buttermilk
1 handful parsley, chopped • 1 small bunch chives, roughly chopped • salt and pepper

1/ Combine all ingredients and purée with a stick blender or food processor.

FOR THE CHICKEN WINGS:
24 chicken wings, pointy bits removed and wings cut in half • 250g butter, melted
1 cup Parmesan, grated • 1 tsp dried origanum • 1 tsp dried chilli flakes
2 tsp paprika • 2 tsp dried parsley • 1 tsp salt • 1 tsp ground black pepper

1/ Preheat the oven to 180°C.
2/ In a bowl, mix the Parmesan, origanum, chilli, paprika, parsley, salt and pepper.
3/ Dip each leg in melted butter, then into the seasoning mixture
and lay in a foiled tray ready for the oven.
4/ Roast the wings until dark and crispy (roughly 40 minutes) and serve hot with dipping sauce.

SERVES 6

COCONUT-CRUMBED WHITE FISH WITH CURRY MAYO

In this recipe you'll learn to crumb using desiccated coconut. If you have
any recipes at home that call for breadcrumbs, you can swap them out
for desiccated coconut. They crisp up exactly the same way as normal crumbs,
only they offer a much nicer nuttier flavour.

FOR THE CURRY MAYO:
½ onion, sliced • 2 tbsp butter • 3 tbsp curry powder • 400ml (one batch) Banting mayonnaise
1 handful fresh coriander • juice of 1 lime • salt and pepper

1/ Sauté the onion in butter until golden brown.
Add the curry powder and fry until the aromas are released.
2/ Scrape the onion and curry mixture into a bowl with the mayo and remaining ingredients.
Blitz with a stick blender and season to taste.

Note: To improve the flavour even more, add a tablespoon of crushed ginger
and garlic to the onions while you fry the curry powder.

FOR THE COCONUT-CRUMBED WHITE FISH:
600g white fish, cleaned, skin off, bones out • 2 eggs, beaten • 2 cups desiccated coconut
1 lemon, cut into wedges • salt and pepper • 80g butter or coconut oil for frying

1/ Cut the fish into 20 to 30g strips.
2/ Place the beaten egg in one dish and the coconut in another. Dip each strip of fish,
one at a time, into the egg and then the coconut. Place the crumbed pieces in a clean tray.
3/ Melt the butter or coconut oil in a frying pan and pan-fry each piece of fish
until golden brown.
4/ Drain on paper towel and serve hot with lemon wedges and curry mayo.
Season with salt and pepper.

Note: For larger batches, you can grill these in advance and warm them
all in the oven before serving.

MAKES 20 PIECES

CHARRED AUBERGINES WITH POMEGRANATE AND TAHINI

This recipe uses aubergines but you could easily swap courgettes into it using the same quantities. The unique, bittersweet, acidic explosion you get in your mouth from the combination of pomegranates and tahini is such a winner!

FOR THE TAHINI SAUCE:
4 tbsp tahini • 1 clove garlic, crushed • juice of 1 lemon
1 handful chives, finely chopped • 2 tbsp double thick Greek yoghurt

1/ Combine the ingredients in a small bowl. While whisking continuously, add drops of cold water one tablespoon at a time until you reach the consistency you like (usually about 100ml of water).

FOR THE AUBERGINES:
500g aubergines, cut into wedges • ½ cup extra-virgin olive oil
3 cloves garlic, crushed • 3 sprigs thyme, chopped
1 handful Italian parsley • ¼ cup pomegranate pips

1/ Preheat the oven to 220˚C.
2/ Get a griddle pan onto the heat at the highest temperature.
While the pan heats up, lightly brush the aubergine pieces with oil.
3/ Grill each piece on each side to get the charred lines and a good smoky flavour.
4/ While grilling the aubergines, combine the oil, garlic and thyme in a small bowl. Set aside.
5/ Once the aubergines are grilled, lay them in a tray and cover with
the garlic and thyme oil. Season with salt and pepper.
6/ Roast the aubergines in the oven for about 15 minutes or until dark brown.
Remove from the oven and leave to cool.
7/ Lay the aubergines on a platter, sauce them liberally with the tahini,
then cover with pomegranate pips and freshly chopped parsley.

Note: Apart from being a knock-your-socks-off item on the grazing table,
these aubergines make for a great side served with lamb of any kind.

MAKES 16 WEDGES

GRILLED MARINATED VEGGIES

Apart from these being excellent on a mezze board or tapas setup, marinated veggies make for very useful staples after the party. Because they suck in all of the oil and are heated, their shelf life is increased by up to two months. By having these in the fridge at all times you can save yourself heaps of time when thinking of what to add to your salad or side veg. You can also use this marinade for olives, simply skip the grilling step.

750g aubergine, courgettes, mushrooms or roasted and peeled peppers (or olives)
2 cups extra-virgin olive oil • 4 cloves garlic, thickly sliced
6 sprigs thyme • ½ cup red wine vinegar

1/ Prepare the vegetables by cutting them into chunks or slices and grilling them on a very hot griddle pan. You don't need to oil them, just grill them long enough to get nice black lines on them. If the peppers are roasted and peeled, you can skip this step.
2/ In a small saucepan, warm the remaining ingredients gently until they become aromatic (don't boil as the oil will change flavour).
3/ Drop the grilled veg into the marinade and leave on a very low heat until warmed through.
4/ Either lay them out on a serving platter or jar them and store them in the fridge.

Note: Charred veggies with marinated feta and fresh mint
is a great-tasting and good-looking platter to put out.

MAKES 1KG

"The only time
to eat diet food
is while you're
waiting for the
steak to cook."

JULIA CHILD

THE SCIENTIST, PROF TIM NOAKES

THE BANTING BLUEPRINT

The biological and evolutionary basis behind the biggest question affecting human health today: what are we designed to eat?

Most of us want to know what we should eat to optimise our health. The answer is simpler than we might think. It is found in the solution to the most important question in the nutritional sciences: why do all mammals not eat exactly the same foods?

Whilst there are obvious anatomical differences between giraffes, koala bears, panda bears, polar bears and lions, the commonalities in their shared biologies are much greater. Yet these similar mammals thrive by eating acacia leaves, eucalyptus leaves, bamboo leaves and shoots, seals, and grass- and shrub-eating game respectively. So rigid are their specific dietary requirements that it requires little effort to discover which foods are best for these animals. Fed on any foods other than those that they naturally eat, all these animals will soon die.

The reason is quite simple: all creatures must eat the foods for which they are designed.

This explains the advantage of the long neck of the giraffe (much better to access the acacia leaves that no other animal other than elephants can reach). Importantly acacia leaves cannot possibly provide all the myriad of nutrients required by the giraffe. It gets these missing nutrients from the hundreds of trillions of bacteria that exist in the giraffe's massive intestine. These life-sustaining bacteria ensure not just the health of the giraffe but also the bacteria's own survival – a perfect symbiotic relationship. But change the giraffe's diet and the key bacteria in its gut will die, followed shortly thereafter by the death of their host. In the same way, the modern diet we've adopted is slowly but surely killing us.

So it follows that if we want to establish which foods are best for modern humans, we need to discover which foods our early human ancestors ate before recent changes in our dietary options, especially those imposed by the Agricultural Revolution that began about 12 000 years ago.

Humans exhibit some unusual physical characteristics; these characteristics tell us much about our unique biology. For our height we have the longest legs of any mammals and the greatest capacity to lose heat from our bodies through sweating. Modern-day elite but tiny human marathon runners weighing less than 60kg can nevertheless sweat at rates of up to three litres/hr during competition. There has to be a biological reason why humans are designed to sweat so vigorously.

We also have (or should have) thin waists and narrow hips that make it easier for us to run long distances without tiring. Humans are also equipped with a complex network of springs in our lower limbs that allow us to store energy in our muscles as our foot lands on the ground when running. That stored energy is then released as the muscles contract, propelling us forward with each stride. This reduces the energy cost of running, improving our efficiency and explaining in part why exercise is not an effective way to lose weight – humans are designed to use energy very efficiently and without waste when we exercise.

A similar network of springs surrounding our shoulders allows humans to throw balls with great velocity and accuracy, just as we once threw rocks and spears.

All these findings suggest that humans are uniquely designed for efficient long-distance running, especially in the heat. Scientists now believe that early humans must gradually have realised that their design allowed them a competitive advantage. For through trial and error they would have discovered that over a period of hours they could effectively chase other non-sweating mammals until those animals became paralysed by heat exhaustion.

At first, because it seems that males became the hunters, early males would have begun by catching the newly-born but defenceless offspring of the smaller antelope on the African plains. As his expertise and courage grew he would have learnt to observe where the leopard stashed its half-eaten prey. Then as a group, many would have discovered how to follow the cheetah and chase it from its recently-caught prey.

But the real advance occurred on an especially hot summer's day when a small band of early humans emboldened by the knowledge that their chief competitor, the lion, was lying somewhere in the shade incapacitated by the heat, set out to chase a much larger mammal like eland or gemsbok, to its exhaustion.

Over time the lean, linear, tall, long-legged, easy-striding modern human became the greatest endurance athlete on the planet. The only mammal, who because of an unmatched ability to sweat profusely from his entire body surface, is able to run without overheating in midday heat. In order to capture and devour the energy-rich bodies of the large non-sweating African antelope, on which humans were so utterly dependent at that time.

The result was, early humans grew strong and clever on an energy-dense diet rich in fat and protein provided by the bodies of savannah-dwelling antelope. But early humans were not yet quite out of the woods, so to speak.

PROTEIN. FAT AND CARBS – a brief history
The Mossel Bay miracle?

Professor Curtis Marean from Arizona State University, USA, believes there is a more recent but yet untold Southern Cape twist to this story. The problem with the popular explanation that the size of the human population has increased progressively over the years, is that it does not explain why, compared to other species, humans show relatively little genetic variation. So little that many geneticists propose that all modern humans are descended from a small band of a few hundred surviving early humans who lived about 195 000 years ago either in east or south Africa. According to Marean's theory, that small band survived the last modern Ice Age by discovering the only remaining site on the entire planet able to provide sufficient food to support their survival – the Southern Coast of Africa, specifically the region around Pinnacle Point near Mossel Bay.

There, modern humans lived in an area bounded on the south and east by the rich Indian Ocean teeming with fish and other marine life, and on the north and west by the land animals that humans had learnt to hunt successfully. Easy access to a bounty of seafood was provided by a severe ice age that locked water at the North and South Poles, lowering ocean levels and exposing the Continental Shelf off the Southern Cape coast for habitation and the gathering of marine food. And underground was the uniquely rich array of bulbs that comprise the Cape Floral Kingdom. The archaeological record suggests that during this period the human brain showed a dramatic increase in size, indicating that in their hardship this small band of humans had discovered a bounty of foods rich in fat and protein, ideal for optimum brain development.

If Marean is correct, it solves the problem of the foods with which early humans developed. We ate a diet rich in fat from fish and pasture-raised animals supplemented by a smattering of carbohydrates from tough fibrous underground bulbs. And those foods would have produced a specific intestinal bacterial flora that thrived on those natural foods and, in turn, optimised human health.

Eventually the Ice Age ended and the progeny of the original humans spread from Africa, crossing into Asia and Europe about 50 000 years ago. At first they would have continued their carnivorous ways, searching for animals rich in protein and fat. In time this would have taken them further north in search of those even fatter animals able to survive the harsh northern winters.

This reliance on animal foods produced a specific human metabolic profile best able to metabolise two of the major dietary macronutrients (fat and protein), but somewhat less well adapted to using the third macronutrient (carbohydrate). This diet, rich in protein and fat but poor in carbohydrate, produces a specific human metabolic profile – insulin (carbohydrate) resistance (IR).

WE NEED TO TALK ABOUT CARBS...

Of the three macronutrients in our diet, only carbohydrate is completely non-essential for life. We cannot function properly for more than a few days without eating fat; without an adequate protein intake we develop protein-calorie malnutrition within a few months. But avoiding carbohydrate has no short- or long-term effects on humans, other than the (usually beneficial) effect of weight loss.

However humans cannot survive without a constant supply of glucose, which is an important fuel for the brain and certain other organs. But this glucose can be produced by the liver from fat and protein and does not need to be ingested as carbohydrate in our diets. We call this process "gluconeogenesis", meaning the production of "new glucose" (that is, glucose that is not ingested but produced from fat and protein).

The amount of glucose we need to produce each day by gluconeogenesis is kept small by our great human capacity to use fats as the preferred fuel for almost all our body's energy needs. The end result is that the majority of humans exhibit a metabolic state known as insulin resistance (IR), present to varying degrees from mild to severe, and in which we exhibit a wide variation in our capacities to metabolise ingested carbohydrate. It is this presence of varying degrees of IR in so many of us that explains why our human health has deteriorated as we have moved increasingly to a diet comprising highly processed foods with carbohydrate as the primary ingredient. Yes, that includes your butter croissant, your ciabatta and your bunny chow.

So this is the downside of our developmental history and the fact that at Pinnacle Point the only carbohydrates we ate were from the fibrous bulbs of the natural Cape Flora, for the carbohydrate in those bulbs is absorbed slowly and does not cause a marked increase in blood glucose and insulin concentrations. In modern terms those bulbs contain carbohydrates that have a low glycaemic index. Humans eating low-glycaemic foods did not need to develop any special biological mechanisms to protect them from high blood glucose and insulin concentrations that you might get from a plate loaded with chips today.

For we now know, not least because of the devastating consequences in those with uncontrolled Type II Diabetes Mellitus (T2DM), that a high blood glucose concentration is very toxic for human tissues because glucose damages the structure of all proteins, the proper function of which are essential for our health. To minimise this effect, the only protective mechanism humans have developed is to secrete insulin whenever carbohydrate is ingested and the blood glucose concentration begins to rise.

Under the action of insulin, ingested glucose is either used immediately as an energy fuel or stored in the liver and muscles. And any carbohydrate that cannot be so removed, must be converted immediately into fat, first in the liver before being transported to the fat tissues for storage as fat. In order to maximise this use of carbohydrate, insulin also prevents fat from being used as a fuel. Hence insulin is the hormone of both fat building and fat storage (by preventing its use as a fuel).

But the efficiency with which these processes occur in each of us is determined by the degree to which we are either IR or its opposite, insulin sensitive.

The degree of IR differs markedly in different humans and in different populations. In its most extreme form, IR is the key abnormality present in T2DM, the form of diabetes that occurs increasingly with older age in persons still able to produce some insulin. (The other less common form, Type I Diabetes Mellitus (T1DM) occurs in persons at a younger age, often children, who lose their capacity to produce insulin usually as a result of viral damage to the insulin-secreting cells of the pancreas. The tissues of T1DM are not necessarily insulin-resistant, although they may be since there is likely a strong genetic predisposition to IR). Those with the most severe IR will develop severe obesity and T2DM at the youngest ages; those with mild IR may notice only that they struggle to control their weight and that their blood pressure tends to rise as does their fasting blood glucose concentration as they pass beyond middle-age.

But perhaps more important is the idea that IR is the hidden metabolic abnormality underlying many of the chronic diseases currently reaching epidemic proportions in modern humans and which includes obesity, T2DM, high blood pressure, high blood cholesterol concentrations and heart disease (Figure 4).

Perhaps the reason why these diseases are now reaching epidemic proportions in all populations eating highly-processed, carbohydrate-rich foods is because those are the exact foods that those with IR are the least able to metabolise safely.

It was this state of IR that best preserved us through those tough years at Pinnacle Point. But when we moved into the Middle East 50 000 years ago, trouble was on the horizon. For it was in the Middle East that humans were to make the first of their two catastrophic modern dietary blunders.

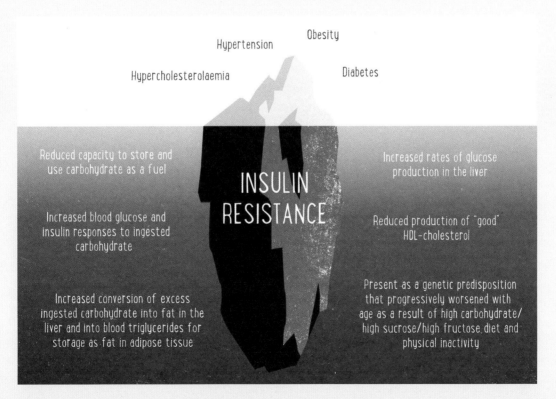

FIGURE 4: Diabetes, obesity, hypertension (high blood pressure) and hypercholesterolaemia are manifestations of a common underlying condition – insulin resistance (IR) – some of the biochemical features of which are shown in this figure. The common treatment of all these conditions is to reduce the daily carbohydrate intake to less than 50 grams/day by Banting.

CARBAGEDDON 1: Farming Fatness

The first great modern human dietary disaster – paradise ends with the invention of agriculture

Beginning about 13 000 years ago, humans living in the Middle East began to domesticate animals and to cultivate grasses, the ancestors of our modern cereals including wheat and barley. In this way cereals and grains were added to the human diet, reducing human reliance on hunting, fishing and gathering.

The exact reasons for this choice remain uncertain – some have suggested that the addictive nature of these grains on the human brain could have played a role. But this dietary revolution produced a dramatic reduction in human health. Compared to the skeletal remains of those who continued to follow a hunting existence, the bones of those who began to eat cereals and grains reveal a sorry story of greatly impaired human health. And the clearest evidence for this can be found in the bodies of the Egyptian mummies.

The Egyptians living in the lush Nile Valley for the 3 000 years between 2500BC and 395AD existed on a diet comprising mainly carbohydrates, especially wheat and barley, which they baked into a flat wholewheat bread. So great was their fondness for bread that Egyptian soldiers were known as "the bread eaters". Egyptian farmers also grew a wide variety of fruits and vegetables, including grapes, dates, melons, peaches, olives, nuts, apples, garlic, onion, peas, lettuce and cucumbers. The result was that the Egyptian diet of that period exactly matched that which would, after 1977, be promoted as the epitome of modern, healthy eating.

In his book *Protein Power*, Dr Michael Eades describes what the Egyptians ate: "[The Egyptian] diet consisted primarily of bread, cereals, fresh fruit, vegetables, some fish and poultry, almost no red meat, olive oil instead of lard, and goat's milk for drinking and to make into cheese – a veritable (modern) nutritionist's nirvana." If such is the ultimately healthy diet "rich in all the foods believed to promote health and almost devoid of saturated fat and cholesterol (and refined sugar)" as we are now taught, then according to Eades, the "ancient Egyptians should have lived forever or at least should have lived long, healthy lives and died of old age in their beds. But did they?"

The mummified bodies of the Ancient Egyptians bear mute testimony to the truth. From their decayed teeth and severely diseased gums, to their obesity, widespread arterial disease and high blood pressure, the bodies of these mummies warn of the dangers of a cereal-based high-carbohydrate diet: "So a picture begins to emerge of an Egyptian populace, rife with disabling dental problems, fat bellies and crippling heart disease… Sounds a lot like the afflictions of millions of people in America today, doesn't it? The Egyptians didn't eat much fat, had no refined carbohydrates… and ate almost nothing but whole grains, fresh fruits and vegetables, and fish and fowl, yet were beset with all the same diseases that afflict modern man. Modern man, who is exhorted to eat loads of whole grains, fresh fruits and vegetables, to prevent or reverse these diseases." Eades concludes that this historical evidence might suggest that "there are some real problems with the low-fat, high-carbohydrate diet."

If only humans had learned from this natural experiment, we might have been spared the second great modern dietary disaster of 1977.

CARBAGEDDON 2: Plumbing New Depths

The second great modern human dietary disaster: the United States Senate Select Committee on Nutrition and Human Needs adopts the 1977 Dietary Goal for Americans (USDGA)

Twelve thousand years later humans were ready for their second catastrophic dietary blunder. Sadly this one should never have occurred since it owes its existence purely to political and commercial factors and a distortion of science on an unprecedented and unimaginable scale. Its key effect was to spread the false gospel that the foods that humans had always eaten had, quite suddenly in the middle of the 20th Century, transformed into the direct cause of all our modern ill-health, most particularly to a rising incidence of heart disease that began after the end of the First World War (1918).

The theory that (saturated) fat in the diet raises blood cholesterol concentration, which then causes heart disease, is known as the diet-heart/lipid hypothesis, also known as the "plumbing theory". It owes its existence principally to the missionary zeal of a single scientist, the American biochemist Ancel Keys (PhD). In 1953 Keys published a scientific paper in which he showed an apparent relationship between the amount of fat in the diet and the heart disease rates in six different countries (Figure 5). He concluded that this proved that by raising blood cholesterol concentrations, the fat in the diet clogs the arteries of the heart and so must be the direct cause of heart disease.

But there were at least four problems with Keys' "science" that continue to go unchallenged by those devoted to his theory.

First, he selected the data from only six of the 22 countries for which he had information. Data from those six countries provided the best visual representation of his theory as they fitted a perfect straight line.

Second, he failed to warn that the simple association of two observations does not prove that they are causally linked. That most men who suffer heart attacks are either bald or have greying hair or both does not prove that grey hair and balding causes heart disease, any more than umbrellas cause rain. Causation can be proved only by randomised controlled clinical trials (RCTs) in which all variables except the one of special interest, are held constant. Keys only ever reported observational studies; he did not undertake a single RCT as truly great scientists must do. For the goal of science is always to disprove that which we hold to be most obviously true. Science advances through disproof of our personal scientific biases. Not through continually "proving" what we already believe to be self-evident.

Thus, in contrast to what many medical students and nutrition scientists are taught, because he did not undertake RCTs, Keys could never prove the diet-heart hypothesis unequivocally.

Third, Keys spent much of his life defending his theory against the criticism that any of a number of other confounding variables could explain, at least as well, the apparently causal relationship he preferred. For example, the single greatest environmental change after the First World War and which could conceivably be the sole important factor explaining the sudden rise in heart disease thereafter, was the growth in cigarette consumption after 1918 (Figure 6). But Keys was on a mission and so he ignored any possible contribution that other factors could have made to the suddenly rising heart disease rates.

Finally, Keys was not a clinician. He did not ever treat a single patient suffering from the disease about which he became the world's leading theorist. Sometimes a little practical knowledge can be helpful.

But Keys was not without critics, the chief of whom was Professor John Yudkin, then Professor of Nutrition and Dietetics at the University of London. Yudkin argued that differences in heart disease rates could as well be explained by differences in annual income between countries; that is, that growing levels of affluence was the real cause of the rising incidence of heart disease. Famously he showed that the rising heart disease rate in the United Kingdom after the First World War was associated with the increasing number of radio and television licences owned by UK citizens. Clearly neither a television nor a radio licence can cause "artery clogging". Yudkin also showed a close relationship between dietary fat and sugar intakes in 41 countries as well as a tight relationship between sugar intake and heart disease rates in the 15 countries for which data were then available. So he argued if countries with the highest saturated fat intakes also have the highest sugar intakes, how is it possible to choose between the saturated fat or the sugar as the "cause" of their heart disease? Then, in a series of research studies, he showed that patients with arterial disease, including those supplying the heart, ate nearly twice as much sugar as did those without those diseases. Others subsequently confirmed an almost perfect relationship between the amount of sugar eaten in different countries and their respective rates of heart disease.

Thus already in the 1970s the evidence implicating sugar as a dietary factor associated with coronary heart disease was at least as strong as that incriminating dietary saturated fat.

But the definitive rebuttal to Keys' false doctrine had been presented in 1957 by two New York scientists, Drs Yerushalmy and Hilleboe. They analysed a wide range of possible associational relationships with heart disease from 22 countries, including the 16 ignored by Keys concluding that: "The evidence from 22 countries for which data is available indicates that the association between the percentage of fat calories available for consumption in the national diets and mortality from arteriosclerotic and degenerative heart disease is not valid; the association is specific neither for dietary fat nor for heart disease mortality. Clearly this tenuous association cannot serve as much support for the hypothesis, which implicates fat as an etiologic factor in arteriosclerotic and degenerative heart disease."

Today we know that the association between the percentage of saturated fat in the diet and the incidence of heart disease in all European countries is inverse (Figure 7) – that is, those countries with the highest percentage saturated fat intakes like France and Switzerland have the lowest rates of heart disease whereas those with the lowest intakes of saturated fat have the highest rates. The Swiss are particularly interesting because they are amongst the longest living people in the world. Yet of all Europeans they have amongst the highest average blood cholesterol concentrations – the opposite of what Keys' doctrine would predict. Indeed there is no evidence that countries with high rates of heart disease have higher average blood cholesterol concentrations than do countries with lower rates of heart disease. In fact the evidence appears to be the opposite (Figures 8 and 9).

Furthermore, grouped analyses of all the published evidence shows that the amount of fat in the diet is unrelated to heart disease risk in individuals and that reducing dietary fat intake over many years does not change heart attack risk. But for those with IR, replacing fat in the diet with carbohydrate is unlikely to be a healthy choice. And even for the healthy, replacing saturated fat with polyunsaturated "vegetable" oils, as promoted by the 1977 USDGA, cannot be healthy because it increases the intake of unhealthy omega-6 and trans-fats whilst reducing the intake of healthy omega-3 fats found in butter and other dairy produce from pasture-raised animals.

Were he alive today, Keys would be unable to produce any of the "proof" that in 1957 he believed to be "unequivocal". In fact all the evidence should by now have finally buried the diet-heart plumbing hypothesis for heart disease. That it has not is because the wealth of the pharmaceutical industry and the modern practice of medicine is crucially dependant on the continued survival of the plumbing theory since without it there is no market for cholesterol-lowering statin drugs.

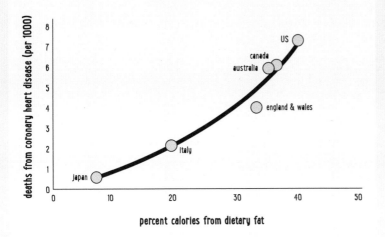

FIGURE 5: In 1952 Ancel Keys PhD published a paper apparently showing a strong linear relationship between the amount of fat ingested by the citizens of 6 different countries and the incidence of heart disease in those countries. This iconic figure was used as "proof" of the still unproven theory that especially fat in the diet causes heart disease. This study shows an association between two variables. But associational studies prove absolutely nothing.

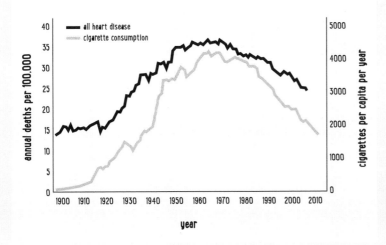

FIGURE 6: The annual number of deaths from heart disease in the United States began to rise shortly after the end of World War I. The rise and subsequent fall in heart disease deaths nicely tracks the rise and fall of cigarette consumption. Smoking is one of the most potent causes of heart disease so that these two events could be causally related. Instead, led by scientists like Ancel Keys PhD, after 1953 the US decided to find a specific nutritional cause for the rise of heart disease ignoring any potential role for changing smoking patterns in the US. Fat, especially saturated fat was the chosen nutritional villain even though the consumption of saturated fat in the US has been falling since the early 1900s. But the consumption of sugar and polyunsaturated "vegetable" oils has increased exponentially over the same time period.

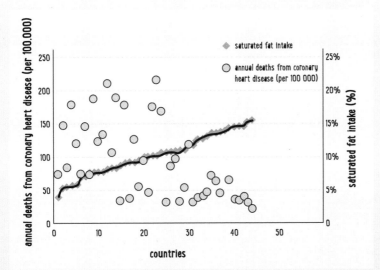

FIGURE 7: The annual number of deaths from heart disease in each of the European countries is an inverse function of the percentage of daily calories derived from saturated fat so that countries (like France and Switzerland) that ingest the most saturated fat have the lowest annual heart disease death rates. This is sometimes known as the "French Paradox". But it is not a "French Paradox". It is better termed the "European Paradox".

But might this European data showing an inverse association between saturated fat in the diet and incidence of heart disease (Figure 7) support an opposite theory; specifically that saturated fat in the diet protects against heart disease?

Perhaps, but no credible scientist today would perpetuate Keys' cardinal error of claiming that association proves causation. If differences in heart disease rates between European countries are indeed due to dietary and not other factors, then perhaps they are due to differences in consumption of the "healthy" foods that we have been told to eat instead of fat. These include especially sugar, high fructose corn syrup, cereals and grains and other refined carbohydrates, and vegetable oils. An increased consumption of any or all of these rather than more saturated fat in the diet, could well explain this apparently paradoxical relationship.

The real tragedy is that the removal of fat from the human diet, as advocated by Keys and his disciples, is very likely the single direct cause of the obesity (Figure 10) and diabetes epidemics that began after 1980. Which raises the question: why did these twin epidemics begin in 1980? And not before, or after?

The industrialisation of corn production in the United States after 1970

Just as Keys was formulating his false theory, political events were conspiring that would expedite the global expansion of his false diet-heart hypothesis. In 1972, US President Richard Nixon was confronted with a losing and increasingly unpopular war in Vietnam, by rising food prices and by a disgruntled farming community. He appointed Earl Butz as Secretary of Agriculture with two orders: bring down the price of food and increase the wealth of US farmers. Butz decided that the production of corn and soy on an industrial scale by farmers working as a huge conglomerate and receiving large state subsidies was the solution to both "problems". His actions would have momentous effects on global health. Perhaps if there is one single person we can blame for the current obesity/diabetes epidemic, it is Secretary Butz (with help from "Tricky" Dick Nixon).

The industrialisation of corn and soy production would be of little value if all the newly grown grains were not eaten, first by US citizens and their livestock and then by the rest of the world. But how to convince the world that grains and cereals are healthier than the foods high in protein and fat that previous generations of healthy Americans had always eaten? Enter Senator George McGovern and his side-kick, vegetarian Nick Mottern.

THE 1977 DIETARY GOALS FOR AMERICANS (USDGA)

After a series of cursory interviews with selected scientists, in 1977 Senator George McGovern and his Senate Select Committee on Nutrition and Human Needs released the first Dietary Goals for Americans (USDGA). These novel guidelines driven by powerful commercial and political forces to ensure the growth of US farming through the industrialisation of corn and soy production, were based entirely on Keys' unproven and subsequently disproven diet-heart hypothesis. These new guidelines mandated "healthy" Americans to restrict their intake of saturated fats and cholesterol (in eggs) and instead to base their diets on at least eight to12 servings of grains and cereals per day. These grains and cereals, foreign to all humans until as recently as 12 000 years, would replace the high-protein and fat foods like butter, lard, milk, cream, cheese, eggs and meat that until then had been the American staples. Instead those were relegated to the third tier of the soon-to-become ubiquitous Food Pyramid (Figure 11) that has dominated the teaching of human nutrition ever since.

These 1977 USDGA guidelines, compiled by the vegetarian Nick Mottern who had no formal training in nutrition science and who selected only the expert information that fitted his personal conviction, were criticised by Dr Philip Handler, then President of the National Science Academy (NSA). Handler who noted: "Resolution of this dilemma turns on a value judgement. The dilemma so posed is not a scientific question; it is a question of ethics, morals, politics. Those who argue either position strongly are expressing their values; they are not making scientific judgements."

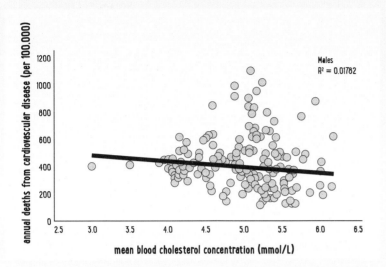

FIGURE 8: Cardiovascular disease death rates and mean blood cholesterol concentrations for men in 171 countries sampled by the World Health Organization.

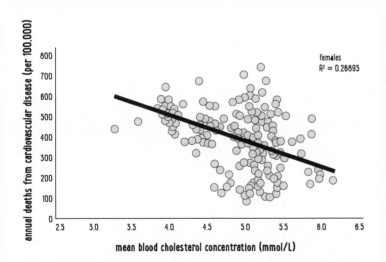

FIGURE 9: Cardiovascular disease death rates and mean blood cholesterol concentrations for women in 171 countries sampled by the World Health Organization. Note that in both Figures 8 and 9 the relationship is inverse. That it the higher the blood cholesterol concentrations. the lower the cardiovascular disease death rates. Total mortality showed exactly the same relationship. falling as a linear function of increasing blood cholesterol concentrations. The findings in Figures 7. 8 and 9 refute absolutely the false diet/heart hypothesis of Ancel Keys.

Similarly, a leading cholesterol expert of the time, Professor Eric Ahrens noted that "This illogic is presumably justified by the belief that benefits will be obtained, vis-à-vis CHD prevention, by any diet that causes a reduction in plasma lipid (cholesterol) levels."

The Food Pyramid and these untested guidelines were soon promoted and supported by a range of other US Government agencies, not least the National Institutes of Health (NIH), which began to focus increasing amounts of its research budget to provide the definitive "proof" that persons who followed the 1977 USDGA would become immune especially to heart disease, obesity and diabetes. Note that the function of research organisations like the NIH is to support research that aims to disprove, not to prove, existing "truths".

Unfortunately the three major research projects funded by the NIH over the past 40 years – the Framingham Study, the Multiple Risk Factor Intervention Trial (MRFIT) study and the $700 million Women's Health Initiative Randomised Controlled Dietary Modification Trial (WHIRCDMT) – all failed spectacularly to "prove" that this dietary change produced significant health benefits. The most interesting of these studies is perhaps the WHIRCDMT, the goal of which was to determine whether post-menopausal women who adopted a "heart healthy" low-fat diet, high in vegetables, fruits and grains, reduced their risk for developing cardiovascular disease (CVD). The trial substantially favoured the intervention group who also received an intensive nutritional and behaviour education programme not offered to the control group. This diet is exactly that which made the Ancient Egyptians so ill. Had the NIH scientists understood the archaeological record, they could have saved $700 million. Imagine if these scientists had chosen rather to study the diet that healthy Americans had favoured for the three centuries before the heart disease "epidemic" began after 1918 (Figure 6).

The authors' conclusion after 8.1 years of study was that: "… A reduced total fat intake and increased intake of vegetables, fruits, and grains did not significantly reduce the risk of coronary heart disease (CHD), stroke or CVD in postmenopausal women and achieved only modest effects on CVD risk factors." In fact this study made a number of inconvenient discoveries that the authors glossed over.

First, post-menopausal women with heart disease at the start of the trial had a 26% increased risk of developing heart disease during the trial if they adopted the "healthy" low-fat diet compared to women who continued to eat the traditional unhealthy diet with a higher fat content. Second, women who were either lean or middle-aged at the start of the trial were more likely to gain weight during the trial if they ate the low-fat diet. Third, the healthiest women were more likely to develop diabetes if they reduced the fat in their diet, whereas the condition of those with established diabetes was also more likely to worsen if they did the same.

Within five years of the widespread adoption of these new dietary guidelines, global rates of diabetes and obesity increased explosively, especially in the United States. The damage caused by the adoption of the 1977 USDGA began to appear quickly. By 1994 American men had increased their daily energy intakes by 22% and American women by 6% (Figure 12). Beginning after 1980 there was also an immediate (8% in men and 9% in women) increase in the rates of obesity in the USA within the same 14 years (Figure 10), perfectly matching this increased intake of calories, especially from carbohydrate.

Any increased intake of carbohydrates by those with IR (Figure 4 on page 259) would be more than enough to explain the simultaneous rise in global obesity and diabetes rates. This tight linkage by both time and plausible biological mechanism between the increased carbohydrate intake promoted by the 1977 USDGA and the rising incidence of obesity and diabetes after 1980 is the final evidence we need to prove that these dietary guidelines have had a catastrophic effect on global health.

CARBAGEDDON 3: frankenfoods

The third catastrophic modern human dietary disaster: genetically modified foods.

Modern carbohydrate food sources differ substantially from those tough fibrous Cape Floral bulbs on which the pioneering humans survived at Pinnacle Point 200 000 years ago. Today especially the sweetened fruits and carbohydrate-rich vegetables that we eat bear no resemblance to those less sweet and poorly digested foods that existed in nature at the time of the Agricultural Revolution. The result is that modern

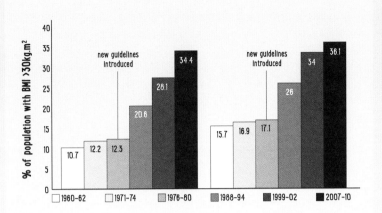

FIGURE 10: The rising incidence of obesity in the US begins in 1980, 3 years after publication of the 1977 USDGA which promoted the removal of fat from the diet and its replacement with (fattening) carbohydrates. (From http://www.cdc.gov/nchs/nhanes.htm)

FIGURE 11: The Food Pyramid promoted by the 1977 USDGA. The pyramid relegates the foods traditionally eaten to the third tier replacing them with 6-11 servings a day of foods that were first introduced to humans only ~12 000 years ago and which were followed immediately by a reduction in human health, best exemplified by the diseased bodies of the Ancient Egyptian mummies.

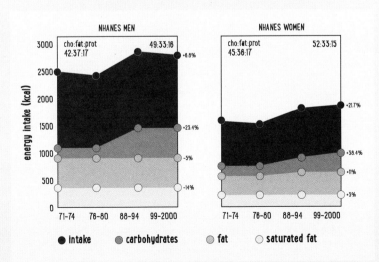

FIGURE 12: Changes in the intakes of the three major macronutrients – carbohydrate, protein and fat – and of total calories in men (left panel) and women (right panel) before and after the promotion of the 1977 USDGA and the Food Pyramid. Note that calorie and carbohydrate intakes were stable from 1970-1980 but rose thereafter following the adoption of the 1977 USDGA. The increased consumption of calories from carbohydrate matches exactly the increasing rates of obesity (and diabetes) beginning after 1980 (Figure 10). This effect is explained by the stimulatory effect of carbohydrates on hunger and hence on increasing calorie consumption. (From Hite et al. 2010)

fruits and vegetables have a higher usable carbohydrate content that is rapidly assimilated within the human body. This causes a steep rise in blood glucose concentrations, setting off a steep increase in blood insulin concentrations especially in those with more marked levels of IR. In addition the fruits that were available at Pinnacle Point were seasonal, unlike the modern provision of fruits all year round.

In the last few decades the cereal and grains that constitute the 6-11 servings that we are encouraged to eat daily (Figure 11), have undergone substantial genetic modification, not to improve our health, but to increase their profitability. As a result, a typical slice of modern bread raises the blood glucose and insulin concentrations as quickly as the same weight of glucose. By raising our blood glucose and insulin concentrations so rapidly and repeatedly, modern bread is killing us just as surely as did the cereals and grains favoured by the Ancient Egyptians.

WHY DOES GOOD FAT GET A BAD RAP?

Re-establishing balance: The growth of low-carbohydrate eating with reversion to our ancestral eating patterns

Chefs, it seems, know best when it comes to what we should be eating.

The first person to suggest that a high-carbohydrate diet promotes weight gain was French gastronome Jean Anthelme Brillat-Savarin. In 1825, Brillat-Savarin concluded that: "All animals that live on farinaceous (starch-rich) substances become fat; man obeys the common law" so that as "farinaceous food produces fat in man as well as in animals, it may be concluded that abstinence from farinaceous substances tends to diminish embonpoint (plumpness)." Brillat-Savarin's thinking had perhaps been influenced by his escape from Paris to New York in 1793 to evade the Christian persecution. He was surprised by the plumpness of the New Yorkers and wondered if this was due to either their Dutch heritage or the "extraordinary amount of pastries, pies, sweets and corn products eaten." But it was not Brillat-Savarin who would be immortalised for this insight that carbohydrates, not fats, make humans fat. That honour belongs to an unlikely Englishman, the formerly chubby William Banting.

A GRAVE UNDERTAKING

In 1862 Banting, a well-connected and prosperous London undertaker, self-published the first edition of his 14 page Letter on Corpulence, Addressed to the Public in which he described his lifelong battle with obesity and its apparently miraculous cure following the adoption of a novel eating plan prescribed by his ENT surgeon, Dr William Harvey. Banting had consulted Harvey to find a cure for his growing deafness. Harvey concluded that Banting's problem was that his obesity was causing pressure on the nerves in his ears. Not aware of Brillat-Savarin's conclusion, Harvey had decided independently that a diet containing "farinaceous" foods was fattening, so logically the avoidance of starchy foods was the key to the treatment of obesity.

Banting's Letter on Corpulence sparked unprecedented public interest. But Harvey's dietary advice was initially shunned by the medical community as he was unable to explain why his treatment was effective. In time he proposed that the inclusion of generous amounts of protein, not the avoidance of carbohydrate, produced this dramatic weight loss. As a result he modified the original diet to include more protein and less fat, a change which Banting considered inferior to the original (higher fat) version. Instead a German physician, Dr Wilhelm Ebstein, became the principal advocate of the original low-carbohydrate, high-fat (LCHF) moderate protein version of Banting.

Acceptance of Banting spread throughout Europe and was initially promoted in the United States by Dr William Osler, Professor of Medicine at Johns Hopkins University in Baltimore, USA. Osler is an iconic figure in global medicine as he wrote the world's first medical textbook evaluating how effective the array of medical treatments available in 1892 were. His conclusion: not very.

Yet in his iconic textbook Osler prescribed the high-fat version of Banting as the treatment for obesity. So in the words of perhaps the most famous medical practitioner of all time:

"Many plans are now advised for the reduction of fat, the most important of which are those of Banting, Ebstein and Oertel. In [Banting] the amount of food is reduced, the liquids are restricted, and the fats and carbohydrates excluded."

"Ebstein recommends the use of fat and the rapid exclusion of carbohydrates… Farinaceous and all starchy foods should be reduced to a minimum. Sugar should be entirely prohibited. A moderate amount of fats, for the reasons given by Ebstein, should be allowed" (p. 1020).

The point is that the very first diet books ever published assumed it self-evident that carbohydrates cause obesity and that carbohydrate restriction is the only treatment for obesity. Hence one must conclude that eating plans for weight loss that are not based on carbohydrate restriction can legitimately be labelled as "fad diets" since they are different from those adopted as effective by the medical profession.

Banting was also promoted in the US by the writings of archeologist Vilhjalmur Stefansson, who had lived with the Arctic Inuit for more than a decade, sharing their exclusive fat/protein diet. On his return to the US, Stefansson wrote a book, *Not By Bread Alone* and became the subject of a year-long laboratory trial during which he avoided all carbohydrates including vegetables and fruits, essentially recreating life on the Arctic Tundra. Despite the researchers' certainty that he would likely die from scurvy, Stefansson quickly lost two kilos in the first week and a further two kilos within the first month, remaining in perfect health for the duration of the trial. His experiences inspired a long lineage of low-carbohydrate diets, which Stefansson labelled consecutively the Eskimo Diet, the Friendly Arctic Diet, the Blake Donaldson Diet, the Alfred W. Pennington Diet, the Du Pont Diet and the Holiday Diet. The popularly maligned Atkins (1972) diet is just one of the most recent examples in this 150 year lineage of low-carbohydrate eating that begins with Harvey and Banting. In fact there are now probably close to 100 books that have been written about Banting, with most appearing in the past five to seven years.

Unquestionably it is Dr Robert Atkins' *Diet Revolution*, published in 1972, that has been the most influential of all these books. Unfortunately for Atkins his book appeared at the exact moment that President Nixon, facing re-election, had decided to increase the wealth of US farmers and bring down the price of food, by industrialising the production of grain. Clearly there was no place for an upstart New York doctor to be telling Americans that they should rather eat the foods that Americans had always eaten – meat rather than maize; saturated fat rather than grains.

If Atkins made one substantial error it was that he failed to undertake clinical studies on the more than 60 000 patients it is estimated that he treated for obesity and related conditions at his New York clinic over the four decades that ended with his death in 2003. Only shortly before his death, perhaps after he had contracted a form of heart disease caused by a viral infection, did he encourage and fund a group of scientists led by Drs Jeff Volek, Stephen Phinney and Eric Westman to study the effects of his diet on various health parameters. This work has established that the Atkins diet consistently outperforms the diet based on the 1977 USDGA in all parameters measured. Unfortunately this information has yet to become part of the mainstream teaching in either medicine or the nutritional sciences.

THE BUTTERFLY EFFECT

How a seemingly arbitrary policy decision in 1970s America has catapulted humanity into health decline and nutritional chaos.

By reducing "artery clogging saturated fats" overstuffed with calories, the USDGA's decision in 1977 was meant to prevent both heart disease and obesity. But as so often happens when theories are accepted on the basis of incomplete evidence, there is the probability that unintended consequences will result. The epidemic of obesity and diabetes that began after 1980 is a classic example. But how do we explain it? To understand it, we need to meet the principle player.

MEET THE APPESTAT – the most important part of your body you've never heard of.

The appestat is the part of the brain, situated in the hypothalamus, thought to control the regulation of human body weight. Just as a thermostat controls temperature, the appestat controls your appetite.

Any explanation of why humans have grown so fat quite recently must explain two irrefutable facts. First that for almost all of our existence, humans have been lean. It's only recently that we've become podgy, overweight and obese. This tells us that the natural state of humans is to be lean. We simply responded to the normal biological cues that accurately regulate our energy (food) intake so that it matches precisely – to the final calorie – the amount of energy we need to sustain our daily physical activity and the integrity of our bodies.

This process is known as the homeostatic control of body weight through the precise matching of energy intake and energy expenditure. Some liken this control to the action of an appestat in the brain that regulates our appetite so that we are always just hungry enough to eat the exact number of calories that we need each day.

It follows that since humans have grown increasingly fat after 1980, then the cause must be damage to the appestat. If we understand what has damaged the appestat, we understand what is causing the modern obesity epidemic.

An important clue is that the increase in obesity (Figure 10) occurred immediately after humans began to eat more carbohydrates (Figure 12) and processed foods. That we may also have become less active is irrelevant since a properly functioning appestat simply reduces hunger and the desire to eat in exact proportion to the reduction in energy expenditure.

Since the predicted reduction in daily physical activity since 1980 is the equivalent of about 100 calories/day – about the number of calories present in half a slice of bread – a properly functioning appestat would have had no difficulty reducing our daily food intake by the equivalent of half a slice of bread in order to prevent the obesity epidemic after 1980. Instead, the obesity epidemic is the singular proof that something in our environment has damaged the proper functioning of the appestat.

Since it is much easier to overeat calories in food than to under-expend calories in physical activity, the most probable explanation is that the appestat was damaged by either (i) the increased intake of dietary carbohydrates following the direction of the USDGA to remove fat from the diet after 1977 or (ii) the increased intake of processed foods since 1980. Or a combination of both. (This does not exclude other factors playing a role but they would be complementary, not directly causal).

But how do the experts – the biologists and nutritional scientists – explain the sudden onset of the obesity epidemic after 1980? The answer is that most use the Energy Balance Model of Obesity as the basis for their explanation.

ARGUMENT 1: The Energy Balance Model of Obesity.

This model of human weight control was first promoted in the early 1900s by the German diabetologist Carl von Noorden. He proposed that obesity is due simply to the ingestion of too many calories regardless of whether they originate from fats, carbohydrates, proteins or alcohol. This is best termed the Energy Balance Model of Obesity. An absolute acceptance of this model as the sole explanation for obesity soon gripped the world and lives on as the dominant global explanation. It is the reason why we are told that the sole way to lose weight is to ingest fewer calories, especially less fat, and to exercise more.

According to this model we must regain control of our errant appestats by consciously matching the (reduced) number of calories we must eat each day with the increased number of calories we need to expend in physical activity. The fact that until 1980 the appestat has worked perfectly without requiring any conscious input is conveniently ignored by adherents of this calorie-counting model of weight control. So too is the fact that we can measure accurately the balance between energy intake and expenditure to about 500 calories/day whereas a mismatch of just 10 calories per day will produce obesity over a few years. In fact the only practical measure of calorie balance is our daily weight. If it is stable, our daily energy intake exactly matches our daily energy expenditure.

A key basis for this calorie-counting model of weight regulation is that we control our food intake on the basis of conscious regulators – in other words we can consciously choose to be the weight that we are. As a result if we gain weight it is simply because we have become slothful and gluttonous – we actively choose to do too little exercise and to eat too much. We lack discipline and motivation.

According to this model, the cause for the global obesity epidemic is really quite simple – it is the result of a massive, global failure of human willpower that began with that generation of humans born after 1980. So if this is the cause, then the solution is also simple. We must regain our resolve; we must correct our suddenly wrong energy balances. By counting our calories, by controlling our portion sizes and by removing fat from our diets, we will again become lean. According to this logic a reduced calorie, high-carbohydrate, low-fat (HCLF) diet of the kind favoured by the Ancient Egyptians will be the most effective weight loss option.

Naturally it is easy to find evidence to support our bias. So we note that the obese are always stuffing their faces and never exercising. And each successive generation is becoming less active and eating more. So the energy balance model is obviously the correct explanation for what we see daily. (What we fail to note is the nature of the foods that the obese eat.)

A key problem with this explanation is that it has proved to be of essentially no practical value. Telling the obese that they are slothful, gluttonous and lacking in willpower and resolve, and putting them on intensive exercise training programmes whilst forcing them to eat a starvation diet (without addressing the composition of that diet) is unhelpful.

We know this because those who try to lose weight according to this HCLF approach show an average weight loss of about 1.5kg despite their best efforts and highest levels of motivation. And when they fail to sustain even that small weight loss, we conclude that this simply proves what we already knew: that the obese are unmotivated and undisciplined. And so we blame the victims for their predicament. Worse, we conclude that obesity is the result of a human character flaw and is incurable. Only the lean are strong willed; all the rest are unworthy of our efforts. Or our understanding.

But the fundamental problem with the energy balance model is that it is brainless – it ignores any potential role for the human brain in regulating both energy intake and energy expenditure. It ignores the role of the appestat that for all but the last three decades of human history has been absolutely precise in directing exactly how much we need to eat each day to keep our bodies at a stable weight. To reverse the obesity epidemic we have to fix the appestat. Dietary interventions based on a brainless energy balance model will never do that since they do not even recognise its existence.

ARGUMENT 2: The Hormonal (insulin) Lipophilic (fat loving) Model of Obesity.

This model is fundamentally different from the energy balance model since it predicts that fat does not accumulate in the body exclusively as a result of an energy imbalance, that is as a simple result of eating more calories than are expended. Rather the model foretells that hormones and especially the fat-building hormone, insulin, are crucial drivers of weight gain. The model also predicts that whilst all calories may be the same when measured outside the body, when ingested, calories from carbohydrate, fat and protein act quite differently. And calories from carbohydrate are uniquely obesogenic (obesity causing) for two different but complementary reasons.

First, carbohydrates stimulate the appetite and encourage the overconsumption of calories; that is calories from carbohydrate act differently on the appestat than do calories from fat and protein. Second, calories from carbohydrate cause increased secretion of the fat-building hormone, insulin, that specifically stores as fat any excess calories ingested as carbohydrate. Third, calories from fat require an input of (wasted) energy before they can be stored or metabolised within the body whereas carbohydrates do not. As a result, calories from carbohydrate are not the same as calories from fat.

This hormonal theory of obesity has its origins in the first half of the 20th century when German scientists realised that persons with T1DM start to lose weight the instant their pancreas fails to produce enough insulin (causing diabetes). Thus it was realised that "a functioning pancreas is essential for the fattening process." They also noted that fat accumulated in specific "lipophilic" areas of the body, more readily in the obese than in the lean. In addition: "Like a malignant tumour or like the foetus, the uterus or the breasts of a pregnant woman, the abnormal lipophilic tissue seizes on foodstuffs, even in the case of undernutrition. It maintains its stock, and may increase it independent of the requirements of the organism. A sort of anarchy exists; the adipose tissue lives for itself and does not fit into the precisely regulated management of the whole organism."

That continues to be well recognised in modern textbooks of human physiology although its relevance has perhaps escaped the attention of medical practitioners and most nutritional scientists. Thus: "Insulin not only promotes fat storage but it also restrains fat mobilisation" and "Lipogenesis (fat storage) is high in the fed state and following carbohydrate administration, whereas it is suppressed by fasting, high-fat diets or insulin deficiency, such as in uncontrolled diabetes."

Unfortunately, the defeat of Germany in World War II and the adoption of English as the universal scientific language buried this theory until it was recently recovered through the remarkable writings of New York science writer, Gary Taubes. Taubes's two recent books *Good Calories, Bad Calories* and *Why We Get Fat and What to Do About It* are perhaps the single greatest reason for the growing academic interest in the insulin theory of obesity and the rise of Banting as the potential solution for obesity. The key benefit of Banting is that being low in carbohydrate, it stimulates neither appetite nor excessive insulin secretion.

The past decade has seen a dramatic increase in the volume of science published on the effects of Banting for weight loss, reversal of risk factors for heart disease and for improving athletic performance, most especially in those with IR. Some of the key studies have been provided by Drs Jeff Volek (PhD) and Stephen Phinney (MD), whose groundbreaking work is summarised in their books *The Art and Science of Low-carbohydrate Living* and *The Art and Science of Low-carbohydrate Performance*. It was these scientists who were the first to be funded by the late Dr Robert Atkins.

As we will discuss subsequently, recent analyses show that Banting is more effective than HCLF in reducing excess body weight and in reversing ALL the established risk factors for heart disease. Since this conflicts absolutely with conventional teaching it is not (yet) easily accepted.

So in summary, the evidence is absolute. The singular and direct cause of the epidemic of obesity and diabetes that began in the first generation born after 1977 was the adoption of the scientifically-unproven 1977 USDGA that encouraged all the world's people to adopt a low-fat, high-carbohydrate diet. This also predicts that each succeeding generation since 1977 will be successively heavier. The biology of this effect is the following:

• Weight gain cannot occur without the ingestion of more calories than are needed by the body. In this sense the energy balance model of obesity is correct. But the point is that the over-ingestion of calories cannot occur if the brain appestat is functioning properly, as it did until 1980.

• The appestat of the obese must fail because it is especially susceptible to the appetite-stimulating effects of high-carbohydrate foods, especially those found in modern processed foods that are designed with the single goal that they are also highly addictive. It is those addictive foods that have invaded the human food chain in the past 30 years.

Next we have the problem of too many IR humans. Eating too much carbohydrate each day will cause weight gain and perhaps even obesity, even in those who are not IR. But according to the hormonal (insulin) model of obesity, weight gain will occur much more easily in those who have an impaired capacity to metabolise carbohydrate because their tissues are IR. Thus in those with IR, carbohydrates are especially obesogenic because every time carbohydrates are eaten, they cause an exaggerated secretion of insulin, which directs the excess ingested calories to be stored as fat. In addition, the carbohydrates specifically cause the overconsumption of calories, not only because they fail to satisfy appetite (as they are usually eaten in foods that are not nutrient dense) but because they actively drive hunger.

MODERN FOOD IS KILLING OUR INNER-CAVEMAN

How a high-carbohydrate diet of addictive foods must cause an obesity and diabetes epidemic in human populations with fragile appestats and varying degrees of IR.

1. EARLY HUMANS REFINED THEIR BIOLOGY IN A LOW-CARBOHYDRATE ENVIRONMENT and only occasionally ate rapidly assimilated carbohydrates (which cause blood glucose and insulin concentrations to rise rapidly, especially in those with IR).

Marean's theory that humans were nearly wiped out as a species and survived only because of the fortuitous presence of the Continental Shelf off the Southern Cape coast helps explain why modern humans are so poorly adapted to eat a diet full of highly refined and easily absorbed carbohydrates. For at Pinnacle Point, early humans enjoyed the bounty of the protein- and fat-rich seafoods harvested with little effort and to which the only added carbohydrate came from the tough fibrous bulbs of the Cape Flora. On this diet we did not need to develop biochemical defenses against sudden increases in blood glucose and insulin concentrations.

We now know that the blood concentrations of both glucose and insulin must be kept as low as possible as both cause long-term detrimental effects. The long-term damage that occurs in diabetes is due to the effect of persistently elevated blood glucose concentrations on many different organs. A key action of insulin is to rapidly lower the blood glucose concentration to limit that damage. But if insulin is persistently elevated, as occurs in those with IR eating a high-carbohydrate diet, the insulin adds to the glucose-induced damage. Insulin is now considered to be an added factor explaining the increased risk for cancer, ageing and dementia in those habitually eating high-carbohydrate diets.

The key action of insulin in the obese with IR unable to burn much carbohydrate as a fuel, is to remove the glucose from the blood stream and convert it into fat in the liver. But insulin also prevents the body from burning that fat as a fuel. So all the extra dietary carbohydrate becomes locked up in the body's fat cells. But dietary fat elevates neither the blood glucose nor the blood insulin concentrations. Protein too has a much smaller effect on insulin secretion than does carbohydrate.

2. HUMANS DO NOT HAVE ANY ESSENTIAL REQUIREMENT FOR DIETARY CARBOHYDRATE.

Humans cannot survive unless they include fat and protein in their diets. But carbohydrate serves only two functions in humans – it must be either burned as an energy fuel or stored as fat; it cannot be used to build any of the body's structures.

This means that the grams of carbohydrate ingested each day must either be used every 24 hours as a fuel or they must be stored either as fat in the fat tissues or as glycogen in the muscles and liver. Persons with IR have a reduced capacity to burn carbohydrate as a fuel both during exercise and when at rest, or to store it as glycogen. Some even argue that storing carbohydrate as fat is the way the human body is designed to cope with a toxic chemical (glucose), which until the Agricultural Revolution was not a major component of the human diet.

Thus the paradox: the single macronutrient, carbohydrate, which has established detrimental effects on our bodies, and for which the human body has no requirement, is the one elevated to the status of a super-health food by the 1977 USDGA.

3. HUMANS DIFFER in the ease with which they will gain weight when exposed to a high-carbohydrate diet.

A large body of scientific evidence shows that IR is the root cause of especially obesity, diabetes, heart disease, high blood cholesterol concentrations and high blood pressure (Figure 4). According to this model, those with the highest degree of IR will develop the visible manifestations of this condition, such as the onset of obesity and T2DM, at the youngest ages.

The prevalence of IR increases with age – in the US it is claimed that 75% of adults over age 65 have IR. The important practical point is the following: persons with IR are never able to eat much carbohydrate if they wish to optimise their health. IR does not improve with age – it is more likely to grow progressively worse.

In the words of Atkins: "As long as you look upon being off your (low-carbohydrate) diet as part of your future plans, you will never solve your weight problem. This can only happen when you accept the reality that if you have a weight problem, you must stay on a diet for life."

His message is simply the following: those with IR can only ever control their weight and health if they restrict the number of grams of carbohydrate they eat each day. This requirement is for life. So Banting cannot ever be abandoned. It must be followed for life.

4. HUNGER IS THE ULTIMATE DETERMINANT OF THE OVERCONSUMPTION OF CALORIES that leads to obesity. So the key feature of the obese is that they are always hungry.

Obesity cannot occur without an overconsumption of calories. And the chief driver of the overconsumption of calories is, not surprisingly, hunger.

Hunger is regulated by two factors in the foods we eat – their bulk and their nutrient density. Bulky foods fill the stomach and produce a rapid satiation whereas nutrient-dense foods turn off hunger for much longer. Importantly, carbohydrates and protein/fat foods act quite differently on both these directors of our hunger.

Carbohydrate-rich foods like pasta, potato, cereals, bread and many vegetables are bulky and when eaten they quickly fill the stomach, producing a more immediate satiation. But because these foods are not nutrient-dense, their satiating effect passes quite quickly and hunger returns usually within an hour or two. As a result, most people eating high-carbohydrate diets must eat every three hours as they are continually hungry. In this way, repeated ingestion of high-carbohydrate foods encourages a high calorie intake even in those who try to eat less by denying their hunger. In contrast, foods with high nutrient density satiate hunger over much longer periods – six to 12 hours.

So the key discovery when persons change from eating carbohydrate-rich but nutrient-poor foods to nutrient-dense "real" foods of the kind that we have always eaten is that within a few days, hunger disappears. Instead with hunger satiated, we are freed to eat only when circumstances are right – that is, when the right foods are available.

5. ADDICTIVE FOODS PRODUCE CONTINUAL HUNGER and so are the key drivers of the obesity/diabetes epidemic.

Investigative reporter Michael Moss has provided a game-changing book entitled *Salt Sugar Fat: How the Food Giants Hooked Us*. The book contains two key revelations.

The first is that Moss describes how the manufacturers of processed foods use a special testing method to identify the "bliss point", which is the "precise amount of sugar or fat or salt that will send consumers over the moon". So processed foods are engineered specifically to maximise their addictive potential, to ensure that we will always "crave" these fake foods.

To compound the problem, the industry uses other "devious moves: lowering one bad boy ingredient like fat while quietly adding more sugar to keep people hooked". In other words, labelling unhealthy high-sugar, processed foods as "healthy, low-fat" options.

Moss' second revelation is the one with which he begins his book – a meeting in Minneapolis in April 1999 when the 11 men who control the US processed food industry met to hear Michael Mudd, vice-president of the company Kraft, speak about "childhood obesity and the growing challenge it represents for us (the processed food industry) all". Mudd's simple conclusion was that these men and their industry are to blame: "What's driving the increase (in childhood obesity)?" His answer: "Ubiquity of inexpensive, good-tasting, super-sized, energy-dense foods."

And his suggested plan of action to reverse the problem followed logically from that conclusion: "The industry should make a sincere effort to be part of the solution (of the childhood obesity problem). By doing so, we can help to defuse the criticism that's building against us. We don't have to singlehandedly solve the obesity problem in order to address the criticism. But we have to make a sincere effort to be part of the solution if we expect to avoid being demonised."

To do this, he suggested, the industry would have to reduce the addictive nature of the foods they produced and to stop driving overconsumption through devious advertising and marketing.

The response to Mudd's plea was direct and unambiguous. It came from Stephen Sanger, then head of General Mills, a company that was then generating $2 billion a year from the sale of sugary breakfast cereals. "Don't talk to me about nutrition. Talk to me about taste, and if this stuff tastes better, don't run around trying to sell stuff that doesn't taste good." And with that the processed food industry in the US turned its back on any possible role it might have in causing the global obesity and diabetes epidemics. In essence it decided that its responsibility was to generate profits. Not to worry about the health of those using its products.

In 2013, following the publication of Moss' book, Mudd wrote an article in the *New York Times* in which he said: "Confronted with this [claim that their industry is driving the obesity epidemic], the executives who run these companies like to say they don't create demand, they try only to satisfy it. 'We're just giving people what they want. We're not putting a gun to their heads,' the refrain goes. Nothing could be further from the truth. Over the years, relentless efforts were made to increase the number of 'eating occasions' people indulged in and the amount of food they consumed at each."

It is a socio-political-economic problem that began with the desire of certain US politicians to ingratiate themselves with their housewives (by producing cheaper foods) and their farmers (by subsidising the production of maize and soy). This led to the growth of the processed food industry, the profitability of which is driven by cheap, addictive, long-lived, high-carbohydrate foods that humans find irresistible.

The result is that for the first time in our 3.5 million year evolution, after 1980 humans began to eat more calories than they require for their optimal health. And as a consequence, they grew fat. The only reasonable prediction is that unless there are some radical reforms, led by the world's politicians, humans will continue to grow even fatter with each succeeding generation.

Since the obesity/diabetes epidemic can only be solved by those governments that are prepared to legislate against industries producing those addictive foods that are driving the epidemic, the world's politicians have a simple choice: continue to allow the unrestrained production and marketing of the processed foods that are the direct cause of the growing obesity/diabetes epidemic, in which case governments will have to invest exponentially more money in treating the medical consequences of that choice. Or promote the provision and consumption of real foods with the ultimate elimination of highly addictive processed foods. This will cause the loss of jobs and tax revenue but will dramatically improve the nation's health whilst reversing rising medical costs. So the money saved on sustaining a nation's ill health can be used to grow a truly healthy and productive nation.

The nations that first take this radical step will be those that dominate our collective global future.

SOMETHING TO DIGEST

It is now clear that the "experts" who told us that energy-dense high-fat foods cause obesity were under influence from the US government in its desire to change the nature of the foods eaten. Since US scientists are more credible than those from any other country, this advice was quickly accepted as the global "truth".

Independent scientists warned of the danger of undertaking an experiment without knowing what would be the most likely outcome. For example, Dr Philip Handler, then director of the National Academy of Sciences asked: "What right has the government to propose that the American people conduct a vast nutritional experiment, with themselves as subjects, on the strength of so very little evidence?"

Similarly the opinion of a leading cholesterol expert of the time, Dr Eric Ahrens was: "... A trial of the low-fat diet recommended by the McGovern Committee and the American Heart Association has never been carried out. It seems that the proponents of this dietary change are willing to advocate an untested diet to the nation on the basis of suggestive evidence obtained in tests of a different diet."

Sadly the results of that experiment are now all too obvious (Figure 10). The experiment failed. It is time to acknowledge the error and to start healing the world.

THE SOUTH AFRICAN EXPERIMENT

How 127 brave Banting guinea pigs turned their lives and their health around and kickstarted *The Real Meal Revolution* in South Africa.

As described in my book *Challenging Beliefs*, in December 2010 I embarked on a personal experiment to start Banting. The results were so spectacular that I decided to speak about them publicly a year later. This soon became something of a national issue and many in both the medical and dietetics professions were less than happy with my successful weight loss following my dietary conversion. Some wondered if I had the necessary qualifications to propound on nutrition; others stated publicly that I had finally lost my senses. A number of leading professional organisations in this country used the public media to warn all South Africans that the "Tim Noakes diet" is dangerous and will damage their health. They were warned that they should most definitely never consider changing their 1977 USDGA "heart-healthy" diet for the dangerous, artery-clogging "Tim Noakes" option.

Nevertheless many thousands of South Africans ignored this advice, choosing rather to experiment along the lines of the simple dietary advice I had posted on the Internet. In time some of those who had experienced successful outcomes wrote to thank me for solving their weight and health problems that the "time honoured" (but unproven) conventional advice had failed to cure. Included in those communications were 127 from subjects who reported the exact amount of weight each had lost. Many included additional health information. An analysis of this information was subsequently published in the *South African Medical Journal*.

The 127 subjects reported a total weight loss of 1 900kg. Remarkably the average weight loss (15kg) far exceeds that usually reported in expensive clinical trials typically involving the HCLF diet under intensive medical supervision and costing many millions of dollars. The data from this simple experiment establishes what well-motivated subjects can achieve in the real world even without supervision, suggesting that Banting is remarkable for weight-loss and health.

By comparison, a combined analysis of nearly 60 000 subjects participating in a number of different studies of the HCLF diet reported an average weight loss of only 1.6kg. Another self-help study of HCLF produced an average weight loss of only 1.3kg at one year and 0.2kg at two years. This evidence confirms that in those who really wish to lose weight by sticking to a few simple rules, Banting is far more effective than HCLF. I now finally understand why this is so. Crucially I would never have reached this insight had I not myself experimented with Banting.

MYTH: YOU ARE FAT BECAUSE YOU ARE A BAD PERSON

For most of the 127 subjects, this was not their first attempt to lose weight and many of them had each tried repeatedly and unsuccessfully to lose weight on a "healthy" HCLF diet. As a result those who were the most overweight had each essentially relinquished any hope of ever again being a reasonable body weight. Billy Tosh's remarkable experience of losing 85kg in 28 weeks is described earlier in this book. Brian Berkman, who lost 73kg when Banting, sought refuge in bariatric surgery from which only his poor state of health saved him. Dr Gerhard Schoonbee, a 57-year old general practitioner who suffered from T2DM, high blood pressure, "high" blood cholesterol concentration, an abnormal heart rhythm (atrial fibrillation) and sleep apnoea, each treated with different medications under specialist care, had informed his wife that he would be dead by age 65. On HCLF he had been continuously hungry and unable to sustain any significant weight loss nor reverse any of his five potentially fatal medical conditions. Yet when Banting he quickly lost 25kg and cured all his conditions so that he no longer requires the use of any medications. A 23-year-old mother, who developed gestational diabetes during her first pregnancy, had tried numerous different weight-loss methods, all of which had failed as she would eventually "cheat" and regain any lost weight. She had never been informed of the addictive nature of her food choices. Yet as soon as she began Banting she lost 45kg in 10 months. Despite significant training volumes, Simon Gear, could not prevent a progressive weight gain with age. After adopting Banting his weight loss was greatest when he exercised the least.

But if sloth and gluttony alone cause obesity, then none of these subjects should have been able to reverse their obesity since such character defects are presumably immutable. That 127 subjects reported large weight losses confirms that this remarkable weight-loss response to Banting is not restricted to a few "biologically abnormal" human variants.

Crucially, a large number of respondents spontaneously indicated that they had never been able to lose weight and keep it off as effortlessly as with Banting. What might explain this unexpected response?

BANTING ACTS BY REDUCING OR REMOVING HUNGER

Through my personal experience while Banting I discovered for myself that the key determinant of whether a particular eating plan will produce successful long-term weight loss is, unquestionably, the extent to which the new diet reduces hunger and as a direct consequence, caloric intake. Twenty-seven of the 127 subjects spontaneously reported that their symptoms of hunger were dramatically reduced or absent when Banting. This was most obvious in the cases of Billy Tosh and Brian Berkman, who lost 85 and 73kg respectively when Banting, without hunger, despite eating only a fraction of the calories they had previously needed to satisfy their food cravings (and addictions).

So the key to the remarkable efficacy of Banting appears to be its capacity to produce satiation despite a reduced energy intake. In contrast, the hypocaloric HCLF diet usually fails because it produces the opposite – increased hunger. As Professor John Yudkin noted in 1958, "The high-fat diet is in fact a low calorie diet."

Indeed it was Yudkin who first documented what I have termed the "Yudkin paradox". In 1970 Yudkin and his colleague Dr Anne Stock reported a study in which they switched the diets of 11 subjects from a typical "heart-healthy" 2 330 calorie/day HCLF diet providing 216g/day of carbohydrate (57% of total calories) to one in which they could eat as much as they liked provided they restricted their carbohydrate intake to less than 70g/day. Remarkably when eating to hunger when Banting, the 11 subjects spontaneously reduced their total calorie intake to 1 560 calories/day, a reduction of 33% (770 calories). Analysis also found that total fat and protein intakes did not change when converting from HCLF to Banting. Thus the only change was a 150g/day reduction in daily carbohydrate intake.

Stock and Yudkin also reported: "In conformity with our experience with [Banting] during the last 15 years, none of our subjects complained of hunger or any other ill effects; on the other hand, several volunteered statements to the effect that they had increased feeling of well-being and decreased lassitude."

It is the removal of carbohydrate from the diet that reduces hunger– not the provision of more calories from fat. Thus carbohydrate stimulates appetite – it does not reduce appetite. Whereas the HCLF diet stimulates your hunger, making you want more. Banting treats your hunger rather than stokes it.

Other health benefits: Banting cures some cases of T2DM, high blood pressure and "elevated" blood cholesterol concentrations. Following adoption of Banting, 14 subjects with T2DM reported that they no longer require medications to control their abnormal blood glucose concentrations, indicating that Banting "cured" their T2DM, an outcome which years of expensive pharmacological intervention had been unable to achieve in some. A further eight with T1DM or T2DM were able to reduce their use of diabetic medications following the adoption of Banting.

The finding that Banting improves glucose control more effectively than HCLF in those with impaired carbohydrate metabolism is established although seldom acknowledged. Instead South African patients with either type of diabetes are usually encouraged to eat diets in which carbohydrate provides at least 40% of daily calories and more than 130g/day. It is not proven that this is the best advice.

Historically, before the discovery of insulin, patients with T1DM were managed on very high-fat carbohydrate-restricted diets since "carbohydrates taken in the food are of no use to the body and must be removed by the kidneys, thereby entailing polydipsia, polyuria, pruritus and renal disease."

Eight of the 127 subjects reported that the adoption of Banting cured their high blood pressure (hypertension); another seven were able to reduce their anti-hypertensive medications after Banting. Another five subjects reported that their "elevated" blood cholesterol concentrations had normalised so that they no longer needed to use medication.

This suggests that along with its remarkable effects in morbid obesity, Banting should be considered as a treatment option to cure T2DM, hypertension and "elevated" blood cholesterol concentrations in some without the need for life-long medication. This is important since modern pharmaceutical agents can cure none of these conditions.

But what these findings really prove is that obesity, T2DM, hypertension and "elevated" blood cholesterol concentrations all have a common cause: a high-carbohydrate diet in those with IR (Figure 4). Understanding this explains why Banting can cure all these conditions.

DUTY BOUND
Why Banting can no longer be ignored in South African Medicine and Dietetics.

Rule 27A of the Guidelines for Good Practice in the Health Care Professions issued by the Health Professions Council of South Africa states that "a practitioner shall at all times... provide adequate information about the patient's... treatment alternatives, costs associated with each such alternative and any other pertinent information to enable a patient to exercise a choice in terms of treatment and informed decision-making pertaining to his or her health and that of others" (p. 20) [emphasis added by current author].

The publication of this study backed by an extensive body of literature confirming that Banting is effective in the management of obesity, diabetes, high blood pressure and high blood cholesterol concentrations requires that South African practitioners, both doctors and dieticians, now have the ethical responsibility to offer Banting as an option to any patient who qualifies.

This is in keeping with the landmark decision of the highest Swedish medical authority, the Swedish National Board of Health & Welfare, which, after a two-year investigation, concluded in January 2008 that "low-carb diets can today be seen as compatible with scientific evidence and the best practice for weight reduction for patients who are overweight or have T2DM, as a number of studies have shown effect in the short term and no evidence of harm has emerged…"

FREQUENTLY ASKED QUESTIONS YOU MIGHT HAVE

FAT VS HEART ATTACKS
But won't I die from a heart attack if I eat all that fat?

Recall that the false idea that we should eat less especially saturated fat came from Ancel Keys' erroneous belief and ultimately his dogma that fat in the diet is the singular cause of heart disease. We now know that saturated fat is unrelated to heart disease risk in individuals. Nor is there any evidence that saturated fat intake predicts heart disease rates in different countries. Instead any relationship (Figure 7) appears to be the reverse of what Keys supposedly found (Figure 5). Similarly the evidence appears to be that countries with higher blood cholesterol concentrations have lower rates of heart disease than those with lower blood cholesterol concentrations (Figure 8 and 9).

In the end Keys' failed "plumbing model" of heart disease has proved too simple to be true. For example, Keys' explanation is that saturated fat in the diet is converted directly into "cholesterol" in the blood stream, which then passively "clogs" the arteries just as might a drain pipe become "clogged" after years of continual use. But human arteries are not inanimate pipes. Nor is it plausible that a substance (cholesterol) is produced by our livers with the sole purpose of clogging up our arteries. Human biology simply does not work that way. If cholesterol is produced by the liver and transported in the blood to all the cells of the body, it is because it must serve an important purpose. Indeed cholesterol is one of the most critical chemicals in the body and humans could not survive without it. Without cholesterol, human life is impossible. To provide its life-sustaining actions, cholesterol is transported to all the body's cells to supplement the cholesterol that each produces for its survival.

The first challenge to Keys' theory arose when early epidemiological studies showed that those with higher concentrations of one form of cholesterol, HDL-cholesterol, had a lower, not a higher risk for developing heart disease. This was a disturbing finding.

But the "experts" soon came up with a simple explanation. From henceforth cholesterol would be classified as either "good" or "bad". Whilst HDL-cholesterol may be "good", the other major cholesterol constituent, LDL-cholesterol, must be "bad". According to this simplistic interpretation, "artery-clogging" LDL-cholesterol is the "bad" form in which cholesterol is produced by the liver and then transported to the arteries where it is free to do its "artery-clogging" damage. In contrast the "good" HDL-cholesterol removes some of the cholesterol from the arteries and returns it to the liver (where it can immediately be turned back into "artery-clogging" LDL-cholesterol to be returned to the arteries in order to repeat the endless process of arterial damage and disease promotion. The illogic of this explanation of how HDL-cholesterol can be "good" seems to have escaped the attention of those who prefer this explanation.

But cholesterol is neither "good" nor "bad". It is just cholesterol. And anyone who continues to use this simplistic terminology exposes his or her ignorance.

The truth is that cholesterol does not even exist in the blood as a fat. Instead cholesterol is insoluble in water (and blood) because it is a fat. So it can be transported in the blood only in a water-soluble form. This is achieved by covering the cholesterol with a protein lining. In this way cholesterol in the blood is in fact a protein, not a fat. The technical term is that cholesterol is transported in the blood as a class of proteins known as lipoproteins. Certain lipoproteins are indeed linked to an increased risk of heart disease and so some lipoproteins are indeed "bad". But the simplistic focus on blood "cholesterol" as the key risk factor for heart disease is not just wrong, it is also bad for our health. For it leads directly to the wrong conclusions of which diet is best for the prevention of heart disease. Only when we understand the contribution of the different lipoproteins to our risk of developing arterial damage and heart disease can we begin to understand which diet will ensure our optimum health and minimise our risk of developing heart disease.

In the first place it is biologically impossible for humans to convert saturated fat into "bad" LDL-cholesterol. There is simply no biochemical pathway that allows this to happen. So Keys' explanation that saturated fat in the diet causes heart disease by increasing LDL-cholesterol production should have been thrown out as a biological impossibility in the 1950s. Instead it continues as the dominant teaching, because the pharmaceutical industry determines what is taught about heart disease in medical schools. Since cholesterol-lowering (statin) drugs are one of the most profitable groups of pharmaceutical agents, the industry has no appetite for anything other than that the simplistic "plumbing" model of heart disease should be taught to medical students or believed by all medical doctors.

Second, the "bad" lipoproteins as well as all the other risk factors for heart disease are affected to a far greater extent by the carbohydrate than by the fat content of the diet, regardless of how much saturated fat is ingested. To understand this we need to understand in much greater detail the way in which the risk factors for heart disease (and other chronic illnesses) interact and how they are affected by either the carbohydrate or fat content of the diet.

IF FATS NOT TO BLAME. WHAT IS?
If bad cholesterol is not the direct cause of arterial damage and heart disease. then why is cholesterol found in diseased arteries?

The "plumbing" model of heart disease states that "bad" LDL-cholesterol damages arteries in direct proportion to its blood concentration; the higher the concentration, the worse the arterial disease. According to this explanation, "bad" LDL-cholesterol simply crosses into the arteries when its blood concentration rises above some critical value – usually above 2-3mmol/L.

But there are a number of flaws with this simple explanation. First, arteries are naturally impervious to the entry of cholesterol. Second, human arterial disease is highly selective; it occurs typically only in short sections of the (damaged) arteries and never affects veins, which constitute a major portion of the vessels in human circulation. This shows that something other than simply the blood cholesterol concentration determines whether human blood vessels will or will not be damaged.

Third, the majority of persons who develop heart disease in countries like the US have blood LDL-cholesterol levels below the cut-off value considered to predict freedom from heart disease risk. Similarly, the majority of persons with "high" blood LDL-cholesterol concentrations will never suffer a heart attack.

The alternate explanation is that arteries are damaged by the entry of only one form of lipoprotein, the small, dense LDL-cholesterol particles, and then only if those small, dense LDL-cholesterol particles have been damaged by becoming oxidised. It is proposed that oxidised small, dense LDL-cholesterol particles have the ability to enter damaged arteries where they become "stuck" within the arterial wall, inducing an inflammatory reaction that leads ultimately to the irreversible arterial damage recognised as arterial plaque.

Thus according to the explanation, it is not "cholesterol" that causes arterial damage but rather the entry of small, dense, oxidised LDL-particles into arteries.

Since diets high in carbohydrate or fat have opposite effects on the blood concentrations of "cholesterol" and small, dense LDL-cholesterol, the diet that appears optimum for health will be different depending on whether you believe it is "cholesterol" or small, dense LDL-cholesterol particles that cause arterial damage and heart disease.

(i) FACTORS PREDICTING RISK OF FUTURE HEART ATTACK

The most recent (Di et al. 2012) analysis of the risk factors that, according to the "plumbing" model, predict future risk for heart disease are listed in Table 1. In that table the "risk" factors are listed according to the relative strength of their ability to predict future risk of heart attack. For example a Relative Risk of 2 indicates that that risk factor predicts a two-fold increased risk of heart disease or a 100% increase compared with a factor that added no risk and so had a Relative Risk of 1.

Table 1: Hazard ratios for seven factors considered to predict future risk for the development of coronary heart disease.

Risk Factor	Hazard Ratio (Relative Risk)
Diabetes	2.04
Age	1.87
Current smoking	1.79
High blood pressure	1.31
Total blood cholesterol concentration	1.22
Blood triglyceride concentration	1.19
Blood HDL-cholesterol concentration	0.83

Of these factors, only diabetes, age and current smoking are the more powerful predictors. An elevated total blood cholesterol concentration predicts only a 22% increased risk of heart disease that, according to the nature of these predictions, is almost meaningless. In fact of all the factors only one, diabetes, really stands out as a powerful predictor of heart attack risk. It is also known that the increased risk of heart attack in diabetics is not explained by higher blood LDL-cholesterol concentrations since their values are no higher than those without diabetes who also develop heart disease.

(ii) Why do abnormalities in carbohydrate metabolism elevate the risk of arterial damage and heart disease in persons with IR and T2DM?

It is the abnormally elevated blood glucose concentrations (Figure 3) that explain why diabetics are at such high risk for developing arterial damage leading to heart disease.

A key finding is that the single best predictor of heart attack risk is the blood concentration of glycosylated haemoglobin (HbA1c)(Figure 2). The blood HbA1c concentration is a measure of the average blood glucose concentration over the previous 12 weeks. It is an indicator of the extent to which elevated blood glucose concentrations have damaged key body proteins by adding glucose (glycosylation) to any proteins in direct contact with the blood. Glycosylation alters protein function, making them less effective in their various functions. Since haemoglobin is one of the most abundant proteins in blood, the extent to which it is glycosylated gives a good indication of the extent to which other critical body proteins have been damaged by too high blood glucose concentrations.

Figure 2 shows how the Relative Risk for coronary heart disease events – including heart attacks – and for deaths from all-causes (all-cause mortality) rises with increasing blood HbA1c concentrations. Note that HbA1c values above 6.4% are associated with a sudden exponential increase in risk for heart disease and all-cause mortality so an HbA1c value in excess of 7% is associated with a seven-fold higher risk for a coronary heart disease event. Compare this to the 1.22-fold increased risk for a heart disease event if one has a "high" blood cholesterol concentration (Table 1).

Another study reported the cumulative incidence (%) of coronary heart disease (Figure 3: Left panel) and of heart attacks (Figure 3: Right panel) as a function of a random blood glucose concentration measured at any time during the day. It shows that by age 60, 30% of those with random blood glucose concentrations greater than 11mol/L (indicating the presence of T2DM) had already been diagnosed with coronary heart disease, whereas only by age 80 had the same percentage of those with a random blood glucose concentration below 5mmol/L received the same diagnosis. The right panel of Figure 12 shows that by age 93 only 30% of those with a blood glucose concentration below 5mmol/L had suffered a heart attack whereas already by age 68, 30% of those with blood glucose concentrations greater than 11mmol/L had suffered the same fate.

This evidence suggests that high blood glucose concentrations are the single most important factor predicting risk that arterial damage causing heart disease will develop. It seems that glucose damages arteries directly through the glycosylation effect on key proteins and also by promoting oxidation of the small, dense LDL-cholesterol particles.

Another piece of the puzzle comes from the same study showing the ability of elevated HbA1c concentrations to predict future heart attack risk. That study also included two other measures of blood fat concentrations, blood HDL-cholesterol and blood triglyceride concentrations (Figure 13). The data showed that subsequent mortality over the 12 years of follow-up in the study in both men (left panel) and women (right panel) was least in those who had a combination of high blood HDL-cholesterol concentrations and low blood triglyceride concentrations (top lines) and was worst (bottom lines) in those with the opposite – low blood concentrations of "good" HDL-cholesterol and high blood triglyceride concentrations.

The factors linking these findings are the following: high-carbohydrate diets in those with IR cause elevated blood glucose concentrations and high HbA1c concentrations, ultimately leading to T2DM. But high-carbohydrate diets also cause elevated blood triglyceride concentrations and lower HDL-cholesterol concentrations in those with IR.

Thus the common factor linking the findings in Figures 2, 3 and 13 are high-carbohydrate diets in those with IR/T2DM.

(iii) The studies of Drs Jeff Volek, Stephen Phinney and Eric Westman show that all risk factors improve on a low-carbohydrate diet.

Dr Atkins began to fund the research of Drs Volek, Phinney and Westman shortly before his death. The result is a body of novel information best captured in their excellent books *The New Atkins For a New You*, *The Art and Science of Low-carbohydrate Living* and *The Art and Science of Low-carbohydrate Performance*. The results of one of their best studies is shown in Figure 14 which compares changes in a number of blood and other predictors of health in two groups of matched obese subjects who were placed on HCLF or Banting whilst their responses were carefully measured.

The results showed that in all these key variables, Banting subjects showed more advantageous changes than did those assigned to the supposedly more healthy HCLF diet. It is important to note that with Banting, all risk factors moved in the same direction – that is, all improved and the degree of improvement was substantially more than the changes in those following the HCLF diet.

Thus besides greater reductions in body weight and blood pressure, there were greater reductions in parameters of abnormal glucose metabolism, in blood triglyceride and VLDL-cholesterol concentrations (another form of "bad" cholesterol), and small, dense LDL-cholesterol particle numbers, whereas the blood concentration of the "good" HDL-cholesterol concentrations also increased with Banting. This occured without significant increases in "bad" LDL-cholesterol concentrations.

Instead if LDL-cholesterol concentrations rise in Banters, this is due to an increase in the concentration of the large LDL-cholesterol particles, which are not harmful as they can neither be oxidised, nor do they "stick" inside the arterial wall. Thus they do not contribute to the development of the arterial plaque that is the key pathological abnormality in the arterial damage that leads to coronary heart disease.

In contrast, ingestion of an HCLF diet increases fat production in the liver (hepatic de novo lipogenesis – itself a risk factor for arterial damage (see text on page 286), which raises blood triglyceride concentrations and lowers blood HDL-cholesterol concentrations. These responses, the opposite of those occurring in response to Banting, are considered to promote arterial damage and are associated with a reduced long-term survival (Figure 13).

The evidence that Banting produced the greatest benefits in those who are the most ill, like Billy Tosh, is in line with all this evidence and neatly destroys the prejudice that a high-fat diet is a dangerous "fad". Instead the logical conclusion must be that Banting is the safer option for those who are the most ill because they have morbid obesity, diabetes, hypertension and hypercholesterolaemia as a result of more severe IR.

Thus all this evidence suggests that the "healthy" HCLF diet will be much less effective in preventing future heart attacks than Banting and most especially in those with more severe degrees of IR.

(iv) So its not just "good" and "bad" cholesterol.

The finding that the risk factors for heart disease measured by Volek, Phinney and Westman all improved when Banting suggests that we should rather consider risk factors for heart disease as a collective, not simply in terms of either "good" or "bad" cholesterol. Page 286 lists all the important factors that have been identified as predicting risk of future heart attack. I have listed them as markers of abnormal carbohydrate metabolism, abnormal lipoproteins and markers of inflammation.

The point is that these measures give a true indicator of one's real risk of heart disease in a way that the simple measurement of the blood concentrations of "good" and "bad" cholesterol is quite unable. Importantly if many or most of these variables are elevated, it indicates the presence of greater levels of IR and hence an even greater urgency to adopt Banting as a matter of extreme priority. Recall from Figure 1 that IR is the common but overlooked cause for obesity, diabetes, hypertension (high blood pressure) and perhaps elevated blood cholesterol concentrations (hypercholesterolaemia).

MARKERS OF ABNORMAL CARBOHYDRATE METABOLISM

Body weight/body mass index/% body fat
Blood pressure
Blood glucose concentration
Blood insulin concentration
Blood glucose tolerance test (with measurement of insulin concentrations)
Blood HbA1c concentration
Blood ketone body concentration
Blood HDL-cholesterol concentration
Blood triglyceride concentration
Blood uric acid concentration
Presence of non-alcoholic fatty liver on ultrasound

Abnormal Lipoproteins:
Blood concentration and number of small LDL-cholesterol particles
Blood Apo-B concentration

Markers of Inflammation:
Blood ultrasensitive CRP concentration
Blood or tissue omega-3/omega-6 ratio
Blood Fibrinogen concentration – clotting factor

The practical point is that if one wants to understand properly what one's real risk is for developing heart disease some time in the future, then these are the variables that need to be measured. The greater the number of normal results, the lower one's risk, as the fewer abnormalities that are detected, the lesser the degree of IR, which is the real driver of abnormalities in all these tests. On the other hand the greater the number of abnormal tests, the greater the degree of IR and the greater the need to reduce the number of grams of carbohydrate eaten to an absolute minimum, preferably less than 50g/day.

It is not just about heart disease.

T2DM does not only increase one's risk for developing arterial damage and coronary heart disease; those with T2DM are also at greatly increased risk for the development of cancer and dementia like Alzheimer's disease. Is it possible that chronically elevated blood glucose concentrations might also promote those diseases?

The answer is almost certainly yes. For example, a recent study found that elevated blood glucose was a predictor for risk of dementia in both those with and without T2DM; so the higher the average blood glucose concentration, the greater the risk for dementia. So if you want to protect your brain, you need to keep your blood glucose concentration down.

Then there is growing evidence that the key abnormality in cancer is an increased capacity to utilise glucose. In fact, cancer cells do not have the capacity to use any fuel for their growth other than glucose. Unlike the humans in which they occur, cancer cells have an absolute requirement for glucose. Without glucose they starve to death, a point first realised by Dr Otto Warburg, who won the 1931 Nobel Prize for discovering this phenomenon.

Thus the certainty that because they promote the overconsumption of carbohydrates, the 1977 USDGA must also have contributed to the growing incidence of cancer and dementia since 1977.

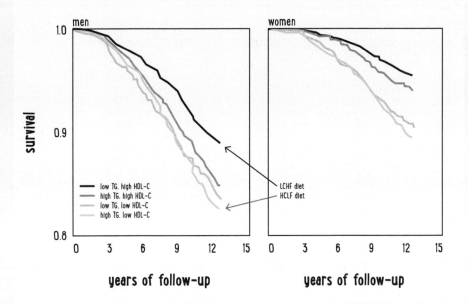

FIGURE 13: Survival curves for individuals with either of 4 different combinations of blood HDL-cholesterol and triglyceride concentrations in men (left panel) and women (right panel). Note that the greatest survival (upper curves in both panels) occurs in those who have a combination of high blood HDL-cholesterol and low triglyceride concentrations whereas the worst survival (lowest curves in both panels) occurs in those with the opposite - low blood HDL-cholesterol and high blood triglyceride concentrations. Interestingly the LCHF diet produces the former (favourable) combination whereas the HCLF diet produces the unfavourable combination of low blood HDL-cholesterol and high triglyceride concentrations especially in those who are the most insulin resistant (Figures 1 and 14). (From Rana et al. 2010)

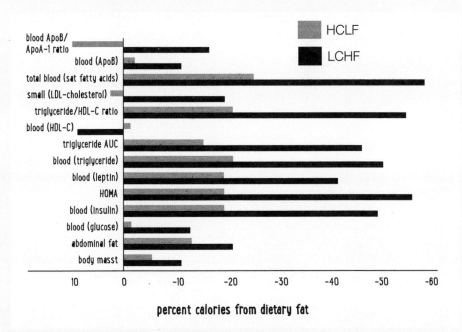

FIGURE 14: The study of Jeff Volek and his colleagues (2008) showed that subjects who lost weight on the LCHF diet showed greater changes in all measured coronary risk factors than did those eating a hypocaloric HCLF diet. Key: ( ) = concentration; AUC = Area Under the Curve; HOMA = Homeostasis Model Assessment; Sat = Saturated. Note that the LCHF reduces, whereas the HCLF diet increases the number of small dense LDL-cholesterol particles that are associated with arterial damage. Total blood saturated fats also fall more on the LCHF than on the HCLF diet. Only the LCHF increases blood HDL-cholesterol concentrations and reduces the blood ApoB/ApoA-1 ratio.

index

a

ADHD 36-37, 44
adrenal function 37
agriculture, impact of 20, 259-260, 264
Ahrens, Eric 265, 277
alcohol 50
allergies 40
almond
> dressing 214
> and strawberry smoothie 103

America *see* United States Dietary Goals for
> Americans

antibiotics 38
appestat 24, 270-273
Art and Science of Low Carbohydrate Living/
> *Performance, The* 273, 284

asparagus
> bacon, asparagus and soft-boiled eggs 92
> with Parmesan, lemon and olive oil 200

athletic performance 28-30, 256-257
Atkins, Dr Robert 269, 273, 275, 284
Atkins diet 269
Attention Deficit Hyperactivity Disorder (ADHD) 36-
> 37, 44

aubergines with pomegranate and tahini 250
autism 36
avocado
> broccoli and avocado salad 214
> with cream cheese and anchovies 98
> and raspberry shake 103
> salad, avocado, snow pea and mint 222

b

bacon
> with asparagus and soft-boiled eggs 92
> eggs baconnaise 88
> and fat cherry tom with bocconcini 97
> spicy bacon nuts 237

bacteria *see* gut flora
bad breath *see* halitosis
Banting, William 18, 21, 268-269
beef
> and 'cauli-mash' shepherds pie 124
> fat content of 60
> fiery beef salad 122
> lasagne 138
> lime and sumac rump skewers 108
> and lime broth 110
> shoulder, braised 129
> steak with créme fraîche and
> > tomato salsa 118
> 'trinchado' on sauté ed veg 120

Berkman, Brian 278-279
Blaylock, Dr Russell 45
'Blitz Ritz' 98
blueberry and cream cheese hotcakes 101
blue cheese
> dip 246
> and sage roasted gem squash 220

bocconcini, bacon fat cherry tomatoes with 97
bok choi, mange tout and shiitake mushroom
> stir-fry 209

Brandt, Kirsten 43
bread, carb-free 74
breakfast 82-105
Brillat-Savarin, Jean Anthelme 268
broccoli and avocado salad 214
broth
> basic 64
> beef and lime 110
> chicken and coconut 166
> smoky pork 113
> tom yum prawn 178

brussels sprouts with bacon and crème fraîche 205
Butz, Earl 264

c

cabanossi, calamari with olives and 188
cabbage salad with creamy red curry dressing 212
Caesar dressing 164
Cajun rub 154

BIBLIOGRAPHY

Ajala O, English P, Pinkney J. Systematic review and meta-analysis of different dietary approaches to the management of type-2 diabetes. Am J Clin Nutr 2013;97(3):505-516.

Anonymous. The Swedes are eating more butter! eBlogger 2009. http://lowcarb4u.blogspot.com/2009/06/swedes-are-eating-more-butter.html.

Atkins RC. Dr Atkins Diet Revolution. 1st ed. New York: David McKay Company, Inc., 1972:1-310

Atkins RC, Atkins for Life, The Next Level, New York, St Martins Press, 2003.

Banting W. Letter of Corpulence. 3rd edition San Francisco: A. Roman & Co., 1865:1-64.

Bauer J. Obesity: Its pathogenesis, etiology and treatment. Arch Intern Med 1941;67(5):968-994.

Brillat-Savarin JA. The Physiology of Taste. ebooks@Adelaide 2012. http://ebooks.adelaide.edu.au/b/brillat/savarin/b85p/.

Brillat-Savarin JA, Simpson LF. The Handbook of Dining: Or how to dine theoretically, philosophically and historically considered. London: Longman, Brown, Green, Longmans & Roberts, 1859:1-244.

Bueno NB, de Melo IS, de Oliveira SL, da Rocha AT. Very-low-carbohydrate ketogenic diet v. low-fat diet for long-term weight loss: a meta-analysis of randomised controlled trials. Br J Nutr 2013;Epub:1-10.

Coulston AM, Hollenbeck CB, Swislocki AL, Chen YD, Reaven GM. Deleterious metabolic effects of high-carbohydrate, sucrose-containing diets in patients with non-insulin-dependent diabetes mellitus. Am J Med 1987;82(2):213-220.

De Wet N. Are we ready to explore the use of low-carbohydrate diets in the nutritional management of obesity and Type-2 diabetes? SA J Diabetes 2012;Aug:11-16.

Di AE, Gao P, Pennells L et al. Lipid-related markers and cardiovascular disease prediction. JAMA 2012; 307: 2499-2506.

Dukan P. The Dukan Diet. London: Hodder & Stoughton, 2010:1-384.

Eades M, Eades MD. Protein Power: The high-protein/low carbohydrate way to lose weight, feel fit, and boost your health - in just weeks. 1st Edition New York: Bantam Books, 1997: 1-429.

Ebstein W. Fettleibigkeit (Corpulenz). Wiesbaden: J F Bergmann, 1883:1-54.

Falta W. Endocrine diseases, including their diagnosis and treatment. 3rd ed. London: J. & A. Churchill, 1923:1-669.

Fallon S, Nourishing Traditions, New Trends Publishing Inc, 1999

Feinman RD. Fad diets in the treatment of diabetes. Curr Diab Rep 2011;11(2):128-135.

Gardner CD, Kiazand A, Alhassan S, et al. Comparison of the Atkins, Zone, Ornish, and LEARN diets for change in weight and related risk factors among overweight premenopausal women: the A to Z Weight Loss Study: a randomized trial. JAMA 2007;297(9):969-977.

Goodpaster BH, Delany JP, Otto AD, et al. Effects of diet and physical activity interventions on weight loss and cardiometabolic risk factors in severely obese adults: a randomized trial. JAMA 2010;304(16):1795-1802.

Harvey W. On corpulence in relation to disease: With some remarks on diet (1872). London: Henry Renshaw, 1872:1-148.

Haynes, A, The Insulin Factor, London, Harper Collins, 2004.

Health Professions Council of South Africa. Guidelines for good practice in the health care professions: Ethical and professional rules of the Health Professions Council of South Africa as promulgated in the Government Gazette R717/2006. HPCSA 2008. http://www.hpcsa.co.za/downloads/conduct_ethics/rules/generic_ethical_rules/ booklet_2_generic_ethical_rules_with_anexures.pdf.

Heaney, R.P., "Dietary Protein and Phosphorous Do not Affect Calcium Absorption," The American Journal of Clinical Nutrition, 72(3), 2000, pages 758-761.

Hooper L, Abdelhamid A, Moore HJ, et al. Effect of reducing total fat intake on body weight: systematic review and meta-analysis of randomised controlled trials and cohort studies. BMJ 2012;345:e7666.

Hu T, Mills KT, Yao L, et al. Effects of low-carbohydrate diets versus low-fat diets on metabolic risk factors: a meta-analysis of randomized controlled clinical trials. Am J Epidemiol 2012;176 Suppl 7:S44-S54.

Hussain TA, Mathew TC, Dashti AA, et al. Effect of low-calorie versus low-carbohydrate ketogenic diet in type-2 diabetes. Nutrition 2012;28(10):1016-1021.

Joslin EP. A diabetic manual for the mutual use of doctor and patient. Philadelphia: Lea & Febiger, 1919:1-192.

Joslin EP. Pathology of diabetes mellitus. Lecture to the Boylston Medical Society of the Harvard Medical School 1893.

Kendrick, M. The Great Cholesterol Con, London UK, John Blake Publishing Ltd, 2007.

Krauss RM, Blanche PJ, Rawlings RS, Fernstrom HS, Williams PT. Separate effects of reduced carbohydrate intake and weight loss on atherogenic dyslipidemia. Am J Clin Nutr 2006;83(5):1025-1031.

Lennerz BS, Alsop DC, Holsen LM, et al. Effects of dietary glycemic index on brain regions related to reward and craving in men. Am J Clin Nutr 2013.

Mackarness R. Eat Fat and Grow Slim. London: The Harvill Press, 1958:1-128.

Marean CW. When the sea saved humanity. Sci Am 2010; 303: 54-61.

McClellan WS, Du Bois EF. Prolonged meat diets with a study of kidney function and ketosis. J Biol Chem 1930;XLV: 651-667.

Mercola, J The No-Grain Diet, USA, Hodder & Stouten, 2004

Moss M. Salt Sugar Fat: How the food giants hooked us. 1st Edition New York: Random House, 2013, 1-480.

Newburgh LH, Johnston MW. The Nature of Obesity. J Clin Invest 1930;8(2):197-213.

Noakes TD, Vlismas M. Challenging Beliefs: Memoirs of a career. 2nd ed. Cape Town: Zebra Press, 2012:1-392.

Noakes TD. Tim Noakes on Carbohydrates. Health 24 2013. http://www.health24.com/Diet-and-nutrition/Nutrition-basics/Tim-Noakes-on-carbohydrates-20120721.

Nordmann AJ, Nordmann A, Briel M, et al. Effects of low-carbohydrate vs low-fat diets on weight loss and cardiovascular risk factors: a meta-analysis of randomized controlled trials. Arch Intern Med 2006;166(3):285-293.

Osler W. The principles and practice of medicine. New York: D. Appleton and Company, 1978:2-1079.

Paoli A, Rubini A, Volek JS, Grimaldi KA. Beyond weight loss: a review of the therapeutic uses of very-low-carbohydrate (ketogenic) diets. Eur J Clin Nutr 2013.

Petersen KF, Dufour S, Savage DB, et al. The role of skeletal muscle insulin resistance in the pathogenesis of the metabolic syndrome. Proc Natl Acad Sci U S A 2007;104(31):12587-12594.

Promislow, J.H., Goodman-Gruen, D., Slymen, D.J., et al., "Protein Consumption and Bone Mineral Density in the Elderly: The Rancho Bernardo Study," American Journal of Epidemiology, 155(7), 2002, pages 636-644.

Roberts R, Bickerton AS, Fielding BA, et al. Reduced oxidation of dietary fat after a short term high-carbohydrate diet. Am J Clin Nutr 2008;87(4):824-831.

Sandor Ellix Katz, Wild Fermentation, Chelsea Green Publishing Company, 2003

Santos FL, Esteves SS, da Costa PA, Yancy WS, Jr., Nunes JP. Systematic review and meta-analysis of clinical trials of the effects of low-carbohydrate diets on cardiovascular risk factors. Obes Rev 2012;13(11):1048-1066.

Schwarz JM, Linfoot P, Dare D, Aghajanian K. Hepatic de novo lipogenesis in normoinsulinemic and hyperinsulinemic subjects consuming high-fat, low-carbohydrate and low-fat, high-carbohydrate isoenergetic diets. Am J Clin Nutr 2003;77(1):43-50.

Sinclair C, The IBS Low-Starch Diet, United Kingdom, Vermilion, 2003.

Skov, A.R., Haulrik, N., Toubro, S., et al., "Effect of Protein Intake on Bone Mineralisation During Weight Loss: A 6-Month Trial," 10(6), 2002, Obesity Research, pages 432-438.

Spencer, H., Kramer, L., "Osteoporosis, Calcium Requirement, and Factors Causing Calcium Loss," Clinical Geriatric Medicine, 3(2), 1987, pages 389-402.

Spencer, H., Kramer, L., Osis, D., "Do Protein and Phosphorous Cause Calcium Loss?" The Journal of Nutrition, 118(6), 1998, pages 657-660.

Stefansson V. The Friendly Arctic. New York: The Macmillan Company, 1921:1-898.

Stefansson V. The Fat of the Land. New York: The MacMillan Company, 1956:1-339.

Stock AL, Yudkin J. Nutrient intake of subjects on low-carbohydrate diet used in treatment of obesity. Am J Clin Nutr 1970;23(7):948-952.

Taubes G. Why we get fat and what to do about it. New York: Knopf of Random House, 2011:1-257.

Taubes G. Good Calories, Bad Calories. New York: Anchor Books, 2007:1-609.

Taubes G. Diet Delusion, A Knopf, Random House, 2007

Taubes G. The science of obesity: what do we really know about what makes us fat? An essay by Gary Taubes. BMJ 2013;346:13.

Thompson V. Eat and Grow Thin. New York: Cosimo Classics, 2005:1-104.

Tseng, MI, Everhart, J.E., Sandler, R.S., "Dietary Intake and Gallbladder Disease: A Review," Public Health Nutrition, 1999, 2(2), pages 161-172.

Volek JS, Fernandez ML, Feinman RD, Phinney SD. Dietary carbohydrate restriction induces a unique metabolic state positively affecting atherogenic dyslipidemia, fatty acid partitioning, and metabolic syndrome. Prog Lipid Res 2008;47(5):307-318.

Volek JS, Phinney SD. A New Look at Carbohydrate-Restricted Diets: Separating Fact From Fiction. Nutrition Today 2013;48(2):E1-E7.

Volek JS, Phinney SD. The Art and Science of Low-carbohydrate Living. Beyond Obesity, LLC, Charleston, SC. 2011, 1-302.

Volek JS, Phinney SD. The Art and Science of Low-carbohydrate Performance. Beyond Obesity, LLC, Charleston, SC. 2012, 1-162.

Volek JS, Phinney SD, Forsythe CE, et al. Carbohydrate restriction has a more favorable impact on the metabolic syndrome than a low-fat diet. Lipids 2009;44(4):297-309.

Von Noorden C. Obesity. In: Von Noorden C, Hall IW, eds. Metabolism and practical medicine.Keener, 1907:693-715.

Westman EC, Volek JS, Phinney SD. New Atkins for a New You. Vermillion, London. 2010, 1-393.

Westman EC, Yancy WS, Jr., Humphreys M. Dietary treatment of diabetes mellitus in the pre-insulin era (1914-1922). Perspect Biol Med 2006;49(1):77-83.

Westman EC, Yancy WS, Jr., Olsen MK, Dudley T, Guyton JR. Effect of a low-carbohydrate, ketogenic diet program compared to a low-fat diet on fasting lipoprotein subclasses. Int J Cardiol 2006;110(2):212-216.

Yudkin J, Carey M. The treatment of obesity by the "high-fat" diet. The inevitability of calories. Lancet 1960;2(7157):939-941.

Yudkin J. This slimming business. Middlesex, UK: Penguin Books Ltd, 1971:1-208.

http://eatingacademy.com

http://www.carbohydrate-counter.org

http://whatsforsupper-juno.blogspot.com

http://www.thehubsa.co.za/forum/topic/126770-lchf-low-carb-high-fat-diet/

http://www.dietdoctor.com/lchf

http://www.dukandiet.co.uk/en/780.html

http://cavewomaninthekitchen.wordpress.com

http://strictlypaleoish.com/category/lchf/

http://paleospirit.com

http://stalkerville.net

http://paleohacks.com

http://www.lowcarbshighfat.com

http://ditchthewheat.com

http://nourishedkitchen.com

http://www.blogilates.com

www.lchfgourmet.se

www.levamedlchf.se

http://healthyindulgences.net

http://askgeorgie.com

http://www.gfreefoodie.com

http://www.djfoodie.com

http://www.thepaleomom.com

http://hometoheather.com

http://www.allrecipies.com

http://www.elnaspantry.com

http://www.foodnetwork.com

http://www.paleoaustralia.com

REFERENCES FOR FIGURES:

Figure 1: Di AE, Gao P, Pennells L, et al. Lipid-related markers and cardiovascular disease prediction. JAMA 2012; 307: 2499-2506.

Figure 2. Khaw KT, Wareham N, Bingham S, et al. Association of haemoglobin A1c with cardiovascular disease and mortality in adults: The European Prospective Investigation into Cancer in Norfolk. Ann Intern Med 2004; 141: 413-420.

Figure 3. Benn M Tybjaerg-Hansen A, McCarthy MI et al. Non-fasting glucose, ischemic heart disease and myocardial infarction. J Am Coll Cardiol 59; 2356-2365, 2012.

Figure 5. Keys A. Atherosclerosis: a problem in newer public health. J Mt Sinai Hosp N Y 1953; 20: 118-139.

Figure 6. Data from US National Vital Statistics and the Centre for Disease Control and Prevention

Figure 7. From Dr John Biffa: http://www.drbriffa.com/2012/10/02/the-frenchparadox-is-not-a-paradox/

Figure 8. From Dr Richard Feinman: http://rdfeinman.wordpress.com/

Figure 9.   From Dr Richard Feinman: http://rdfeinman.wordpress.com/

Figure 10. http://www.cdc.gov/nchs/data/hestat/obesity_adult_07_08/obesity_adult_07_08.htm

Figure 12. Hite AH, Feinman RD, Guzman GE, et al. In the face of contradictory evidence: Report of the Dietary Guidelines for Americans Committee. Nutrition 2010; 26: 915-924.

Figure 13. Rana JS, Visser ME, Arsenault BJ et al. Metabolic dyslipidemia and risk of future coronary heart disease in apparently healthy men and women: the EPIC_Norfolk prospective population study. Int J Cardiol 2010; 143: 399-404.

Figure 14. Volek JS, Fernandez ML, Feinman RD, Phinney SD. Dietary carbohydrate restriction induces a unique metabolic state positively affecting atherogenic dyslipidemia, fatty acid partitioning, and metabolic syndrome. Prog Lipid Res 2008; 47: 307-318.

conversion charts

LIQUID MEASURE

Standard	Metric
1 teaspoon	5ml
1 tablespoon	15ml
1/4 cup	60ml
1/3 cup	80ml
1/2 cup	125ml
2/3 cup	160ml
3/4 cup	180ml
1 cup	250ml
1 1/4 cups	300ml
1 1/2 cups	375ml
1 2/3 cups	400ml
1 3/4 cups	450ml
2 cups	500ml
2 1/2 cups	600ml
3 cups	750ml

WEIGHT

Standard	Metric
1/2 oz	15g
1 oz	30g
2 oz	60g
3 oz	90g
4 oz	125g
6 oz	175g
8 oz	250g
10 oz	300g
12 oz	375g
13 oz	400g
14 oz	425g
1 lb	500g
1 1/2 lb	750g
2 lb	1 kg

OVEN TEMPERATURES

Fahrenheit	Celsius	Gas mark	Description
225°F	110°C	1/4	Cool
250°F	120°C	1/2	Cool
275°F	140°C	1	Very slow
300°F	150°C	2	Very slow
325°F	160°C	3	Slow
350°F	180°C	4	Moderate
375°F	190°C	5	Moderate
400°F	200°C	6	Moderately Hot
425°F	220°C	7	Hot
450°F	230°C	8	Hot

QUIVERTREE PUBLICATIONS

WRITING JONNO PROUDFOOT ■ PROF TIM NOAKES ■ SALLY-ANN CREED ■ TUDOR CARADOC-DAVIES
RECIPES JONNO PROUDFOOT & DAVID GRIER STYLING AND PROPS CAROLINE GARDNER EDITING TUDOR CARADOC-DAVIES & KIRSTY CARPENTER
PHOTOGRAPHS CRAIG FRASER DESIGN & PRODUCTION LIBBY DOYLE
ILLUSTRATIONS PATRICK LATIMER DTP VICKI SMITH

ISBN 978-0-9922062-7-7

TO GET MORE TIPS, UPDATED INFORMATION, RECIPES AND MORE, GO TO HTTP://REALMEALREVOLUTION.COM

FIRST PUBLISHED IN 2013 BY QUIVERTREE PUBLICATIONS, SOUTH AFRICA ■ SECOND EDITION, QUIVERTREE, 2013 ■ THIRD EDITION, QUIVERTREE, 2014
FOURTH EDITION, QUIVERTREE, 2014 ■ FIFTH EDITION, QUIVERTREE, 2014 ■ SIXTH EDITION, QUIVERTREE, 2014 ■ SEVENTH EDITION, QUIVERTREE, 2014
EIGHTH EDITION, QUIVERTREE, 2014 ■ NINTH EDITION (AFRIKAANS), QUIVERTREE, 2014 ■ TENTH EDITION, QUIVERTREE, 2014
ELEVENTH EDITION, QUIVERTREE, 2014 ■ TWELFTH EDITION, QUIVERTREE, 2014 ■ THIRTEENTH EDITION, QUIVERTREE, 2014
FOURTEENTH EDITION, QUIVERTREE, 2014 ■ FIFTEENTH EDITION, QUIVERTREE, 2014 ■ SIXTEENTH EDITION, QUIVERTREE, 2014
SEVENTEENTH EDITION, QUIVERTREE, 2014 ■ EIGHTEENTH EDITION, QUIVERTREE, 2014 ■ NINETEENTH EDITION, QUIVERTREE, 2014
TWENTIETH EDITION, QUIVERTREE, 2015

15 CLARE STREET GARDENS CAPE TOWN SOUTH AFRICA
TEL: +27 (0)21 461 6808 • FAX: +27 (0)21 461 6842 • E-MAIL: info@quivertree.co.za

www.quivertreepublications.com
Distributed by Quivertree Publications
TO PURCHASE AN IMAGE: www.quivertreeimages.com

QUIVERTREE PUBLICATIONS PLACES GREAT VALUE ON THE ENVIRONMENT. THE PAPER USED IN THE PRODUCTION OF THIS BOOK WAS SUPPLIED BY MILLS
THAT SOURCE THEIR RAW MATERIALS FROM SUSTAINABLY MANAGED FORESTS. SOY-BASED INKS WERE USED IN ITS PRINTING.
EVERY EFFORT HAS BEEN MADE TO ENSURE THAT THE INFORMATION IN THIS BOOK IS ACCURATE. NEITHER THE PUBLISHER NOR AUTHORS
ACCEPT ANY LEGAL RESPONSIBILITY FOR ANY PERSONAL INJURY OR OTHER DAMAGE OR LOSS ARISING FROM THE USE OR MISUSE
OF THE INFORMATION IN THIS BOOK.

ALSO AVAILABLE IN AFRIKAANS

The information and material provided in this publication is representative
of the authors' opinions and views. It is meant for educational and
informational purposes only, and is not meant to prevent, diagnose, treat or
cure any disease. The content should not be construed as professional
medical advice. As the authors are not offering prescriptive or professional
medical advice they cannot be responsible or liable for the decisions and
actions which readers undertake as a result of reading this content. Should
the reader need professional assistance, a qualified physician or health
care practitioner should be consulted.

THE REAL MEAL
REVOLUTION

CHANGING THE WORLD, ONE MEAL AT A TIME